Grounded

To Rennie —
Physician, gentleman,
Saint and one great guy!
Tutto, tutto respeto.
John [signature]

Grounded

John Bogert

Donegal Publishing Company
Los Angeles

❧❧❧❧❧❧

Cover design by Michael Criley - www.michaelcriley.com
Illustrations by Sam Sellers - www.samsellers.com

Donegal Publishing Company, LLC
1850 Industrial Street, #307
Los Angeles, CA 90021
www.donegalbooks.com
Tel: (310) 598-6340
Fax: (310) 349-3441

Library of Congress Control Number: 2010922062
Publisher's Cataloging—in—Publication Data
Bogert, John.
Grounded/John Bogert
1st ed.—Los Angeles, California: Donegal Publishing Company, LLC, 2010
p. cm.
ISBN 13 : 978-0-9788128-4-3
ISBN 10 : 0-9788128-4-0
1. Bogert, John.
2. Journalists—United States—Biography. I. Title.

All Donegal books are available from your favorite bookstore, or from our 24 hour order website: www.donegalbooks.com. Order additional copies of this book at: bogert.donegalbooks.com

This book was written, designed, printed and bound in the United States of America.

To Caitlin, Rachael and Ian

Acknowledgments

I would like to thank Robert Dunne of Donegal Publishing Company for turning a pile of newspaper columns into a book exquisitely wrapped in a cover designed and executed by artist, Michael Criley.

As this book's contents are the product of many years of newspapering, I would also like to thank Daily Breeze City Editor Frank Suraci and all the assistant city editors and news editors who have done such a heroic job of saving me from myself. Notable in that hugely talented pool are Jean Adelsman, Chuck Bennett, Jim Box, C.J. Fogel, Jeannie Grand, Josh Grossberg, Lisa Martini, Jack Mulkey, Rebecca Tubb Mulkey, Verne Palmer, Lisa Reitzel, Judy Sanfield, Phillip Sanfield, Toni Sciacqua and Tony Tranfa. With a special thanks to Breeze Chief Librarian Sam Gnerre, a man of great patience, skill and matchless generosity.

Then there are the people I've loved from the start: Rose Bogert, Josephine DeRosa, Joseph DeRosa, Roseann Keshock and Georgia Mincey. Neither can I forget my great lifelong friends Dick Boling and Ward Brisick. Many thanks also go to Jennifer Huddleston for continually assuring me that reading 6,500 columns wasn't such a big job.

Once again, here's to Caitlin, Rachael and Ian Bogert for loaning me their lives.

Foreword

The garage attached to my dad's house is not just a garage. It is a subdivision for mice—mouse nursery, mouse apartment complex and all-around mouse entertainment center. This sounds disgusting in a HazMat, microbe-and-plague-carrying kind of way. But you've got to hand it to mice; like us, they survive in crippled ecosystems. OK, better than us.

In my Dad's garage is also the usual people-junk: mowers, bikes, tools, and toys—the toys my two siblings and I had as kids, toys that my dad just can't bring himself to throw out. It is almost as if he expects us to return home one day as our small selves and demand this particular Barbie or that special stuffed animal. The man is incapable of disappointing us, even on this level. So the toys remain. After all, you never can tell.

Then there are the bins. It doesn't matter what these bins are made of; the mice are, and always will be, made of stronger stuff. If they want in, they get in. But in this treasure hunt, the joke is on them. The bins contain an incalculable number of copies of the award-winning columns my dad has written over 25 years. The columns were originally published in The Daily Breeze for residents of coastal Los Angeles. As one of his advertising posters once said, "John Bogert: Love him, hate him, read him." People did read the columns; they still do, five times every week. He would never mention this, but I will because I am proud of the guy (as are my older sister and younger brother): His writing has been praised many times over by the L.A. Press Club, the AP News Executive Council of California and Nevada, the California Newspaper Publishers Association and the L.A. Society of Professional Journalists.

But now, those masterful columns are insulation for the rapidly growing mouse community. Since there are over 6,000 of them, the mice have a bonanza of material to choose from. For each of 6,000 days, my dad tried to capture a truth about the human experience—and do it by deadline. He wrote good news and bad news, right and wrong; you know, those dichotomies that are the pulse of the universe.

Writing commentary, profiles, and criticism comes with a problem, though. Today's vital story probably won't sustain that vitality beyond tomorrow. Not much stays meaningful in the long run: No council race will be recalled in a deathbed flashback; grandkids are not told of ballot propositions, nor would they care. So as my dad fished in the Breeze archives for this book's collection, he kept coming back to family and friends, the very people who kept him grounded. Somewhere during this expedition, he discovered that the lighthearted things he wrote about were the most important and universal, the stories about my sister Caitlin, my brother Ian, and me. He also wrote about dogs, friends, hilarious and harrowing events, and, almost always, about love. When you come right down to it, what else in our lives truly endures?

Yes, these stories are ours, but they are yours too. Maybe the details differ, but I think you'll find that the stories are closer to you and your family and your life than you might imagine. Why? Because for all our posturing about our individuality, we all go through the same stuff more or less and all collect our versions of the same stories.

The only difference is, my dad wrote them down on thousand of sheets of newsprint that ended up bundled in our garage. It's his mental and emotional scrapbook, a story of family and of love, all now lying in wait for one more baby mouse needing to be kept warm.

Rachael Rose Bogert

<u>**Grounded**</u>

Contact the author at:
bogert1@earthlink.net

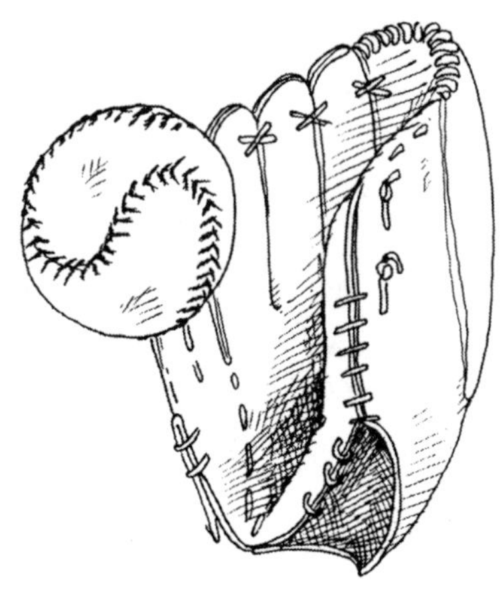

Boys of our summers take last at bats

June 17, 2008

I'm not sure if there is anything as awkward and endearing, as in-between-this-and-that, as on-the-verge-of-something-else as a pack of 14-year-old boys.

Their feet and hands are too large for bodies that insist on remaining thin no matter how many bats are swung and weights lifted. Their hair, for all the effort expended, never quite resembles the 'do they picked out of a catalog at Supercuts.

And their skin, poor things. Their skin alternates between relatively OK to complete anarchy as their innermost hormonal selves work to transform into men the very cores of beings that were recently so small and huggable.

Meanwhile, mothers despair because their baby boys have rejected them, are embarrassed by them. Boys bond naturally with dads, with coaches, with other boys.

To the girls who come to watch them play baseball, the lads seem tribal, insular. They are a raiding party dressed for purposes of the day in St. Louis Cardinals uniforms, even though few of them could find St. Louis on a map.

The girls are, likewise, mysterious. My son and his friend Jack, when I drop them off for Saturday's playoff game—when they remove from the car the great bags containing bats and gloves valuable beyond all ken—they notice the girls.

They could see them from the car standing by the snack bar, walking, cell-phoning, talking to one another, denying the boys eye contact. But they are so obviously there in all their baffling girl glory on a day that is far too hot and sunny for all this.

"Why are they wearing so much makeup?" Jack asks my son.

"Because they're girls," my son replies.

My son has older sisters. He grew up around beautiful girls who treated him like a pet, developing with him relationships that were more girl/puppy than girl/boy.

Still, for all his experience, he can't explain the pretty females who have come to see this game against the Dodgers, this final in the Babe Ruth League playoffs, this winner-take-all, seven-inning test that is itself the end of something in the same way that the girls represent the beginning of something.

This could be the last organized baseball some of these boys will ever play. After today it's high school for all 11 of them. After this it's serious tryouts and cut-lists tacked to locker room walls, the who-goes-away rejection that can linger with a guy for life.

Until now, it has been all acceptance. It started innocently enough, yesterday. Or it seems like yesterday when we put a 5-year-old boy into a Braves uniform and watched him swing and miss at ball after ball. Which might have been less sweetly hilarious had the ball not been perched atop a rubber tee.

But even with the errors that led eventually to something resembling mastery, even with the missed balls going between legs and over heads and the rotten throws to first that invariably resulted in runs, through the tears and smiles, victories and defeats, something was learned by all.

By all I mean the little boys and I mean the guys like me, the dads who deserted the game years ago only to find it—like treasure—exactly where we dropped it.

I'm not talking big leagues here because the big leagues are grand opera. They are big-budget movies, fun to watch but exclusive and so insistent that it's easy to forget that the game still exists at the pure, baggy-pants, kid level same as always—same as a century ago.

For years I'd pass ballfields and see them out there, children and parents engaged in the most American of sports but anonymous and at an emotional remove. Then I came back to it all through a little boy's enthusiasm for a game that he embraced like life itself. Because of him I have a better throwing arm than I did at 13, which isn't saying much aside from how all this is a testament to the game's mysterious ability to draw together father and son with nobody even noticing.

And all along, no matter how we change, no matter how our entire nation changes, the game persists. It's still the same boy vs. boy, bat-on-ball, ball-on-glove contest that drew in the sport's ancients and legends, drawing them in still with the feel of it and the smell of it, with the simple, uplifting attraction of a game whose goal is shaped like a little house called home.

Finally, we have come to this, to this final game, to a moment where there is no anonymity, to a place where no game can be played against any team that doesn't have on its roster five or six mates from past teams, from the

Cardinals, Dodgers, Yankees and Angels of ages 5 to 14.

There's a bond out there among these boys and among the parents, who know that all the freezing evenings, early mornings and blazing hot days on these tatty fields have all been for the present good and for some unknowable future good that may continue well past our time on this earth to include fathers and sons not yet born. Fathers and sons yet to be enthralled by what is good in this game and what is taken from this game into life.

So we lost, 3-2, and trophies were handed out and a final party commenced behind the dugout with barbecue and salads in large aluminum trays. When they finished eating, the kids did what still comes naturally to them.

They retook the red clay field, boys and girls together now, to hit and field and to play with abandon a game older than time itself.

Man's best friend provides final lesson at the end of her life

May 16, 2006

"She's dying," Kathy said, kneeled over our collapsed Rhodesian Ridgeback on Saturday evening. Kathy, a nurse practitioner and a longtime friend, happened to be on hand with a stethoscope to tell me that the lungs in my big dog's chest were suddenly filling and her great heart faltering.

At 14, Cymbre—a kid's takeoff on Simba—was well beyond her life expectancy. A planned and accidental mixture of shorthaired European breeds and the native Hottentot dog that likely gave her breed the wonderful-back-to-front ridge running along their spines, they were bred by Boer farmers in South Africa to protect people and livestock from the lions that some claim they share bloodlines with.

Despite how I brought her home as a whining, wrinkled 2-pound puppy from a local breeder, she carried in that heart an unwavering dedication to home and family. Of course, I know that all the traits we assign dogs are mere hunches. Still, we persist in giving them human characteristics because, after 10,000 years of cohabitation, they are like us.

Or we are like them. Or, in the case of my great hound,

I wish that I was like her. Over all these years I have never met anyone, with the exceptions of a black belt and a Green Beret, born so utterly without fear.

Ten years ago I was followed home by a car containing four tatted-up thugs. Why, I don't know. But there they were suddenly at the end of the driveway with my 12-year-old daughter running in to call the cops and me alone holding a black whiffle-ball bat, the only feeble weapon that came to hand.

Up the drive they came, four guys straight off a pirate ship and me, alone. Then suddenly it was me with my massive beast taking up a shoulders down, fangs bared, drooling, frightening, ridge-on-end position directly in my path.

They had blundered into the very situation this dog was created for. It was like God had put this animal in my path, lending me her absence of fear and the ungodly growl coming from her throat. Strangely, we buy into dog breeds without ever considering the uncommon skills hidden in their genetic memories.

And here she was, suddenly doing her ancient thing, reaching back into her bottomless African heart and holding her ground. And nothing short of death would remove her.

I had to carry Cymbre, all 90 pounds of her, into the house after the pirates ran because she wouldn't release. Nor would she hesitate to stand and place her huge paws on my shoulders when I'd roughhouse with the kids.

It was, or so it seemed, always her duty to protect the small against the big. All along, Cymbre had the back door. She was queen of the garden, the golden-eyed alarm kept alive these last years by my son, who took care of her like a maiden aunt, helping her up on stiff hips and falling asleep nights with a hand on her head.

It was the boy who hurt most when something finally gave out in his big dog. "She was my mom," he said, and it didn't much matter that the world is full of pain and loss greater than this.

Later he'd pull out a stash of photos in which we could see his entire life unfolding beside this dog, with the boy growing tall and his dog going slowly gray but always there at his shoulder, sentinel and guardian.

Cymbre was a present to our daughter on her 6th birthday. Now she's nearly 20, a sophomore at UC Davis and living the small-pet nightmare that comes to so many people her age.

"Somebody is always crying because Skittles or Buddy died," she said, shedding tears for Cymbre. "We got a dog when we were 6. Now the dogs are dying."

With them die huge pieces of childhood and family. Then we see in the flow of memory how silently and completely they have infiltrated our lives through silliness and absolute devotion. And how, as life leaves them in ragged breaths, we might also see a grown man whispering into a floppy ear words of love and thanks.

Spirits soar when old engines roar and nostalgia is revisited

May 15, 1997

It's an obsession with the father's war, with male bonding of a certain kind and with a time and place now unreachable. It is about green aluminum-and-steel, a great B-17 bomber heat-ticking on a runway in smog-ugly Chino.

Mostly it is about collective memory and a plane's massive piston engines turning over, blue-smoking, oil-dripping, straight-piped and vibrating like doomsday. They have the best engine name ever, the Wright Cyclone—four of them bolted way up there on the fat green edges of a magnificent plane called the Flying Fortress.

And let me own up to this once and for all. This is largely boy stuff. Wright Cyclones, the drippy black oil pools beneath them, the clean bite of high-octane aviation fuel, the vision of this wonderful dinosaur prepared to lope across the great basin into Hawthorne Airport—boy stuff, all boy stuff.

Certainly, nothing is more appealing to the boy in us than this plane churning in here now and again, thrilling the old boys who flew them and the younger boys who wish . . . wish for what?

I'll tell you.

They wish for what I am about to do on a hot afternoon after a long, Army Air Corps wait in the wing-shade of a legendary bomber.

They wish, as I do, for make-believe.

Here I am, a man in middle age, a man who never strapped on the armor and fought a good war, a man about to play-act the whole 60-seconds-over-Berlin thing.

Imagine flak, the twin .50s hammering away, the lieutenant up in the Plexiglas nose, eye to the Norden bomb sight at 29,000 feet, up there in the Everest cold, bomb doors open, the plane going suddenly light and turning hard for England.

Only that is garbage. Real boys died in these planes.

On this plane's last visit from its home in Vermont I sat in its belly with men who lost everyone they knew pounding the hell out of Germany. I met a man who sat with an open book listing all the air crews he flew to England with, a book that showed 80 percent casualties.

"Gone," he said, running a finger across yellowing pages, "all gone."

This then is not real except for the real sound of piston engines. On the ground, when planes taxi past, the old war bird lifts on its suspension like a kite. The B-17 being all gun ports and bomb holes, no pressurization, a place for shearling jackets and goggles.

Only today we are playing war at under 10,000 feet in a perfectly restored plane plucked from oblivion.

Of 15,000 made, 12 still fly, still demanding near-constant attention. One hour in the air, 18 in the shop, like the day we all chipped in, struggling under an engine cowling for hours, hand-pumping 50 gallons of oil for the sheer glory of 20 minutes aloft, 20 minutes to buzz Chino airport like olden times.

Which is good because there are men out there who drove long distances with sons and grandsons to lean on canes, to stand for a moment waist-deep in the plane's open bomb bays remembering the heroic moments that once passed for everyday life in a great war.

So this is what it was like, minus the flak and death. It is LOUD, overwhelmingly, earthquake loud with four ominously whirring starters, the big cylinders clearing themselves, catching, vibrating, light lasering in through open rivet holes, prop wash raising the plane like a kite, straining against brakes, then off.

It's a short trip upward, over the Chino dairy cows, over the runway where one can quickly get lost in the Plexiglas nose, out there in the air, ahead of the pilots, between the Wright Cyclones, within the massive noise.

This then is what it's like to fly something awesome.

This is what it takes to make old men come to the perimeter fence, making them hold up small boys like offerings to some ancient sky god, making them marvel for the last time or the first time at something truly grand, something truly worthy, something to make us look up in wonder like our fathers did.

Life in ruins offers notice of what could have been

April 29, 2001

I saw him early on a recent Saturday morning walking down a nearly deserted road. A scarecrow of a man, he staggered along in ragged pants and shirt, shoes back-broken, heels protruding.

He moved with a sideways gait toward the busier cross street below, the street where I live—a nice little life with my family, a nice little life salvaged from a childhood deeply affected by booze. Not that I could say that booze was his problem. But if it wasn't that curse it was another—mental, physical, drugs. We never know anything for certain except the benchmarks of a life in ruins.

The filthy red shirt and trousers, the sad shoes and sidewinder stagger, the eyes focused downward, tripping ever downward while I—citizen and father—do nothing.

Men like this are rare in our neighborhood of good little lives, a neighborhood with scarce foot traffic and closed doors, locked fences, nice lawns and no handouts. In another age, homeless men would come to places like this, leaving arcane symbols on gate posts indicating a soft heart to others of their kind—what was called an easy mark.

But there are no easy marks here now, nothing but a

commonly acknowledged fear on the street I drive toward home. Home to where my little boy watches Saturday cartoons, where my wife sleeps behind locked doors and a home alarm, lollipop signs out front warning of protective electronics within.

I pass and do nothing. Which is not to say that I am not bothered down deep where memories reside of an endlessly compassionate mother—an easy mark if there ever was one—who would feed hungry strangers at her front door. Down deep where the Boy Scout lurks, the altar boy who wanted to save pagans.

That, I think, is partially why I do what I do for a living. Or why I started out in newspapers, later discovering that none of this will ever be enough. On the other hand, this could just be an excuse for not doing everything that I can as I sprint from one goal to the next.

It often seems to me that life is as a high school pal once described it. This pal who bought and sold a little cocaine back in the early '80s, a poor boy who swore he'd stop his illegal dealings as soon as he made his first 100-thou, after he made his first million, his 10th million, until he ended up in federal prison with nothing.

What is it that we need at any given moment. A new car, a better house, better furniture, a college fund, a bigger college fund and a better car until our original good intentions are paved over.

That's life. My life. While the life of that shabby man on the street is not beyond possibility for any of us. Mental illness, addiction, these things strike all of us equally.

So I went back up the street on foot this time.

This time because it is my own neighborhood and not Spring Street or some other place where pain presses in from all sides. I went back with a bag full of juice boxes and protein bars and found the man sitting on a bus bench, rigid, eyes closed, his hands clutching the concrete upright.

He might have been taken for dead were it not for the quivering in his legs. I touch him. His shoulder is flexed, rigid. He is gone from this world. I return home and call 911, where a location is not enough for a matter-of-fact woman who wants a description.

How old is he. Maybe 50. Maybe a lot older. Or maybe younger and worn out. What color is he. He's dark-skinned, maybe black, maybe Latino, maybe Sicilian… how do I know. But I can say that he is the only man passed out on a bus bench within a mile of my home.

The 911 person sounds like she has had a lifetime of messy calls like this, calls that make clean-up crews of cops. A car is on its way, help of a kind. And I return to find the man standing in the middle of the street directing traffic that, in a familiar and disturbing way, is speeding up instead of slowing—zipping past his slight form on both sides.

I wait for a break and step out. I tell him to follow me, tell him that he is in danger, speak right into a face that is trusting and absolutely lost. He follows me to the bench, sits. I poke a straw into a juice box that he sucks greedily like a small boy, eyes closed, as we wait together.

Goodbye, neighbor I never knew

November 15, 1998

He was the older gentleman we'd see around the neighborhood, walking an old dog, scowling, stopping from time to time to berate some innocent neighbor.

I'll call him Mr. Johnson. But I won't speak too harshly of the dead, a circumstance often announced in our staid neighborhood with an estate sale sign hung on a tree. In this case, the sign pointed to a wooden ranch-style setback among too much foliage.

Inside, as Thursday evening closed in around us, two women were trying to get Mr. Johnson's junk out of his house so they could get home to dinner.

"Mind if I look around?" I asked, recalling 12 years of knowing a man that I didn't know at all.

"Mind?" one of them replied. "It's all half-off . . . no, three-quarters!"

And so I was cast adrift in a sea of Mr. Johnson's junk, the life possessions of a crotchety old man who once shouted at my father-in-law over our hedge, "Are you the gardener?"

"No," explained my physician father-in-law. "I'm the doctor."

"In any case," he replied, pointing accusingly at our newly painted melon-colored house, "tell them that their house should be an earth tone." Adding, "And you need to do a better job on these hedges!"

Then came the terrible day when our sheeplike dog, Clifford, sprinted across two lanes of traffic, risking life and fur, for the pleasure of biting Mr. Johnson's sullen beagle Rusty on the butt.

A few days later, Mr. Johnson appeared at my door with a $120 bill for stitches on Rusty's weight-challenged backside.

"I'll accept cash," he announced, finally accepting a check as I joked, "Rusty knows where to find Clifford if the thing bounces."

For years after that, I'd wave and smile. He'd scowl.

Then he died, the estate sellers said, suddenly of a heart attack at 87. Funny, he looked younger, or younger than Rusty, who looked to be about 140. Now here I was with a kind of perverse permission to investigate this two-bedroom junk puzzle, discovering quickly that the guy had been an advertising executive with awards on the wall and a pile of plastic-preserved magazine ads tumbled across the floor.

It was Mr. Johnson's portfolio of ads for shaving creams, hair oils, cars, housing tracts and typewriters, an entire career laid out like a quaint resume, only ghostly because all the products—like the pretty girls and handsome gentlemen posing in them—no longer exist.

Still, they smiled up at me in the Rusty-smelling room, selling me dreams that I could not buy and times past. In the closet hung a World War II Army uniform with captain's bars on the shoulder and two rows of ribbons. Inside the jacket, perfectly pressed, were uniform trousers and shirts. Mr. Johnson also had been an officer and married once until, if the wall photos tell the truth, the mid-1960s.

I could chart the life-course of this good looking young couple—he in that uniform, she a petite blond in white—

growing older in photographic increments. Then their photo life ended like a time-line on a museum wall. No more Mrs. Johnson and no photos of children in between, no further indication of what happened next.

But they did leave behind the stuff of formal entertainment, the cordial and highball glasses, the beer schooners and demitasse spoons of another era, the color television set the size of a computer main frame, the phonograph records he stopped collecting three decades ago.

Over it all was the scent of dust and old dog, of ancient bodies departed and the fragmentary evidence of a life passed between walls now going up for sale. Haul out the junk and the joint is ready for new management—maybe a couple of kids out in that big overgrown yard.

The lesson in all this is obvious and nearly impossible to grasp. When things are gone, they are gone forever.

This is true for Mr. Johnson and Rusty, true for the departed Clifford and true for me. In respect of that I bought a tarnished silver-plated bowl bearing the old man's initials. I bought it to put among my stuff as a reminder.

Remembering Betty, a stepmother who helped a small boy

May 28, 1998

Betty, my father's second wife, began her ghost widowhood 25 years ago.

My sisters knew how she was vaguely and where she was vaguely. But if my late father, who was tossed out of our house when I was 7, occupied the familial hinterland, his second wife inhabited the hinterland's suburbs.

It's a common enough story. A drinking man, the knuckle sandwiches all around, the fear and divorce. But somehow the man was never completely out of the picture.

Out of the pictures, certainly. My mother destroyed all images of the guy, even cutting him out of their wedding photos. I still have one, my mother at 19, small and pretty in satin, in a half photo. She even cut away his hand where it rested on her, excising most of her shoulder in the process like radical cancer surgery.

Still, he would show up when he came down to Florida for the racing season. Nobody especially liked him, but we remained tolerant in a weird Italian familial way.

Betty would always be with him. Betty, my mother told me, was known in a certain part of the upstate New York town where we once lived for "going with men." It was a wonderfully obvious euphemism spoken in a time when "going with men" sounded filthy, in a time when filthy was still possible.

Here's the weird part, I liked her. In a household of pinched pennies, Betty was lady good times. She had sons, she once told me, and loved little boys absolutely. Only nobody ever saw the sons or even heard their names spoken.

It was apparent, especially to me, that Betty wasn't so much showering me with attention as she was recalling these other nameless boys, the ones maybe lost while she was "going with men."

I never told my mother what we did when we were together, my real father and this woman that went with men. What we did was have fun in my father's big old Chrysler, in amusement parks, at the beach and in bars. They'd take me with them, a skinny little kid occupying an honored space as a substitute son with Betty hovering, motherly in roll-and-tuck booths between busty women and hard-eyed males.

When I watch old movies and see the men in overstuffed suits, men perpetually smoking, men absolutely without humor, I recall my father and Betty in bars with their whiskey and me with an orange drink coddled by women who went with men.

And I loved every sleazy, undisciplined moment of it. It was like I had a secret life. Catholic schoolboy by day, junior hood a few times a year with tall, thin Betty hanging on my words, laughing, smoke-hacking at my lame kid jokes, telling me I'm smart like no other adult ever did.

It's all from another age. But I remember all this, and I remember how I wanted a transistor radio back when transistor radios were marvels of expensive miniaturization. And I remember Betty handing me one gift-wrapped, whispering in my ear, "Enjoy."

Only I never knew what parts of that boozed-out life Betty enjoyed or how she seemed to get along with this man who very nearly killed us. I didn't even know she was still alive until my sister faxed me an obituary from an upstate newspaper saying she died at 88 in a home. Not bad, 88, for a woman who smoked and drank like that, a woman who went with men before women who went with men became a fashion.

They listed her maiden name, something else I never heard. She was from Pennsylvania originally and the name was German, like my father's. My father being a German who married disastrously into the whole Italian thing and maybe found something resembling solace in a woman who shared his desperate needs.

It listed no surviving family except parents long dead. Just a few points about a woman who went with men and who was once kind to a small boy, a woman who lived to be 88 and died without a son to comfort her.

A glorious dream of speed and freedom is fading into memory

September 30, 2001

We had serious girlfriends down near Miami, Phil and me.

He would marry his, eventually, and divorce her, eventually. I would eventually drift apart from mine; heartbroken, lost, bereft.

But all that was off in the murky future.

At that moment, in 1969, we were far too busy with the murky present, with hormone rage, with a government that would just as soon have made us soldiers.

What Phil and I had, the only thing we had, were these girls we'd have happily died for. And just as happily cut out for Friday nights for a 350-mile drive down Florida's flat, dark center—past a still Disney-free Orlando, past all sorts of places that would eventually attract hordes of the brain dead and nearly dead.

It was a high-speed turnpike drive through nothing, picking up a toll booth ticket at Yeehaw Junction or some other godforsaken mosquito hummock and flooring it gloriously, endlessly in Phil's Pontiac Firebird. All 400-cubic inches of it, all eight cylinders of it with Holly four-barrels and chrome intake housings—red with a white interior. Or maybe it was white with a red interior. And illegal, since we were college sophomores and forbidden cars.

Phil secreted the snarling monster out near a fraternity brother's apartment, using it primarily for the girlfriend run. Phil and me leaving near sundown. Sometimes we'd have another couple of guys with us, two facing backward, one looking forward with field glasses for the Highway Patrol, for swiveling blue lights, Smokey the Bear hats and the drawl we heard only once.

"You boys know how fast you was going?"

"Yes, sir. Somewhere in the neighborhood of 100 miles per hour ... sir."

The speed was, of course, the insane suicidal attraction of the effort for city boys confined to a countrified college campus, scholastic monks sticking a foot into it and flying south through loamy, cow-scented darkness and open-window orange grove heat. Past places yet to be, from frat house to city via a no man's land that no longer exists in exactly that way.

With that glorious car at the center of it, with eight-track tapes the size of books playing The Byrds, The Rascals and Smokey Robinson so loud it might have kept us awake were we not already supercharged on that Firebird, sister ship to the Camaro. Both of them out of Detroit heaven.

Cars most likely to be bought by guys just back from Vietnam. Wounded and broken and looking for something in those fantastic machines, looking for power and promise, looking at the forward slope of that front end, at the ersatz sports car smallness of the things and knowing in their heart of hearts that it was the exact opposite of what dad would drive.

Back then the overpowered beasts raised eyebrows, made fathers fret when you carted off a daughter in one, leaving entire Asian forests of rubber in the air, clouds of Middle Eastern gas and all the frightful confusion.

Out on the road it was all clear-cut and straight ahead. Four hours with one stop for gas and another halt in Belle Glade to let some freshman off. Then it was the original zoom-zoom down into the human thicket of Palm Beach and Ft. Lauderdale. A million people and two girl-sick boys in a Firebird, the deep-throated roar enveloping us, shielding us.

To this day Phil and I recall the armadillo that crawled out of blackness into the racing spill of the Firebird's headlights, straight over the swamp marsupial and feeling bad about it. But not bad enough to slow down.

Now it's over like a fading dreams, the Firebird and Camaro passing into memory with next year's models. Gone, the car so beloved by so many Italian-American brothers, the car of lesser movie drones, the sports car for people who couldn't afford Corvettes and all the expensive foreign-made stuff that is still more about wishing than owning.

Gone with them is the wonderful low-rent dream of speed and freedom and matchlessly pretty girls waiting just along the road, just beyond where Everglades darkness gives way to heavenly light.

A pang of loss, thinking of a girl, a car and an American century

July 15, 2007

Even now, at an age when this sort of thing is increasingly likely, it was hard to see my first car date listed among the dead on my high school reunion Web site.

There was just a name, Toni Bach, and a picture of her taken in 1967 at the Burdines Department Store studio. In those days, before the art-directed cool-guy color layouts of modern yearbooks, we were all set up for future ridicule—bubble-haired or surfer fluffed—by the same disgruntled photographer.

On sticky south Florida summer days we'd borrow faux gowns or white dinner jackets off hooks in dim changing rooms with Toni surviving all this better than most, looking sharp-eyed and pretty in a picture taken two years after that first date—a date played out in a ratty 1958 Ford that had already been hard-used by two sisters before it got to me salt-corroded with a dashboard sagging from the smacking it took to jerk the radio's vacuum tubes alive.

If it had been any other date in that lost age of dating, in the last moment of a time when boys met parents and opened doors, when home-arrival times were clearly stated and fatherly violence implied, if it had been my third date or 20th, the details would not remain as clear. But there they were waiting to be recognized when I saw her name on a list that included too many good people.

My older cousin clued me in on the firm dad-handshake and mom-compliments, on the back-by-11 promise. I even threw in the name of the movie we were going to, though we didn't go to a movie. What I didn't expect, what delighted me in my nervous state, was Toni standing there in a Villager dress with a smile on her pretty face that begged, "Get me out of here!"

It was a sudden and mutual moment of exultation come to us at the very apex of the American century. We had wheels and we were going out alone in a car for the very first time. I remember Toni wrapping both her arms through mine as we walked away from her front door, away from a beaming mom and a frowning dad, who ran a shoe store and wore a tie in the house. I remember how this girl, who would take such delight in touching pinkies when we passed in hallways, took a small leap into the air.

"We're alone!" she told the warm October night.

I know the date, too, or nearly. I turned 15 on October 7 and this was the following weekend, a meeting arranged even before the state of Florida took my ability to parallel park between concrete-filled barrels and the fact that I hadn't wrecked in two years of provisional driving as proof that I was qualified to hurl around in a 2-ton junker with a 90-pound girl tucked under my skinny right arm.

Sure, it sounds criminal now. But then it felt like we had both been loosed from the chains holding us in a stultifying low-Earth orbit, from an envious year of watching juniors and seniors enjoying lives that resembled Chevy commercials.

She said, "I don't want to waste the night in a movie."

Why sit still when we could drive and drive? Which is

what we did, heading north on the dream highway, A1A, a sandy-shouldered two-lane stretching north past the Kennedy compound in Palm Beach through flat, moonlit, balmy infinity in a Florida that had not yet been loved to death.

With all four windows down and the radio tuned to WQAM Miami, powering past coconut palms and a softly breaking sea, this was surely a hint of the heaven to come.

And I can't recall ever again feeling more in control of my own life and destiny, more in charge and invincible as the salty nighttime wind passed through us like a ghost of possibility.

Like that night, like all things good and bad that we knew so little of, Toni and I didn't last. I don't recall why, exactly, other than we were 15 and convinced of our uniqueness on this Earth.

There was, after all, so much ahead, so many other pretty people and so much to be done, an infinity of things that quickly passed.

Memories of a tree ... and boots

December 21, 2008

It's amazing how we so often miss the importance of events while they are unfolding.

Take nearly freezing to death.

OK, maybe I'm exaggerating. Then again, most events take on certain exaggerated qualities as they graduate from real life, to life lesson, to noble mythology.

Take my mother who, in her 30s, married a complete stranger who was somehow supposed to become my step-dad. But even that expectation paled beside the mystery of why this product of an Anglo-Dutch household would marry my short-fused Italian-born mother in the first place.

He was a widower, gainfully employed and 20 years her senior. She was the penniless divorced mother of three and getting a good deal.

Me, I was the only boy in the father-abandoned bunch, a boy suddenly gifted with a new dad who was quiet to the point of not being there at all. Still, at 7, I was finally getting to do dad-and-son things like throw balls and pound nails into scrap lumber in his basement workshop.

But I didn't make a real connection with him, the connection that would bind us even as he lay dying of unfiltered Camel inhalation, until our great Christmas tree hunt.

Years later I asked him if he remembered that day. He did vaguely. Then again, he wasn't the one who nearly froze to death trailing through snowy New York woods behind a man so quiet he might as well have been a mime.

You see, until stepdad came along, getting a tree usually involved some kind of barter with a fish-eyed guy named Carlo who'd set up a corner lot and spend all his time drinking straight Seagrams 7 and warming himself over a steel-drum fire stoked with sappy evergreen stumps.

But that's not how it was going to work that year, not for a boy whose ship had finally come in. I was heading for a Christmas card scene as the small figure trundling along beside dad as he dragged a freshly cut fire hazard through snow drifts to our cozy country house.

Which was the exact opposite of our grimy mill town reality. Still, I was happy to channel some other kid's life if just for a day, even if it meant going out into snow in city clothes that even I knew were inadequate.

What I wanted were the knee-high, insulated, green rubber, lace-up hunting boots that new-dad wore. What I had were wimpy kid boots that pulled on over street shoes and acted as waterproof refrigerators as long as they didn't take on snow. Then they became blocks of ice.

"Those your best boots?" he asked, lighting his fifth Camel of the morning.

"Yes, but they're good," I replied before quickly changing the subject. "Can I carry the ax?"

"No," he answered, staring out the kitchen window at falling snow like a pilot. "You sure you can take the cold?"

Remember, this was an age when "taking it" was what men did.

"Sure," I insisted, as I watched him expertly pull another Camel out of the pack as we headed out to the Ford wagon.

Soon we were safely past the point of no return. Meaning that today was locked in and it would be our time to share wood lore as we felled a mighty Scotch pine for an otherwise sister-and-mother-infested Christmas.

Along the way I saw a barge icebound on the Mohawk River, and I remember the feeling of freedom I felt when we arrived at the woods.

Falling snow muffled all sound, of car door slamming and new dad talking to the guy he paid. Even our boots sank noiselessly into the white powder as we set out with new dad saying nothing. I guess that I expected more and I expected it to happen instantly.

But the truth was, he could get bad-tempered in his quiet way and he was doing just that as we searched in bitter cold for a tree of proper height.

I played scout dog—running ahead, dropping back, making side trips—but all the short stuff had been walked off. Finally, he decided to fell a tall tree and take its top.

In movies this is easy. In reality, my step-guy had come to parenting late and neither the Camels nor the heavy ax we had carried in were doing him any good as he worked. The longer he chopped, the harder it became for him to breathe. On top of that, my feet were numb inside those cheap boots and I was getting scared.

"What's the matter?" he gasped, finally noticing me.

"Nothing."

"It's those boots, isn't it?"

He finished the tree off and stood it up for my inspection. Standing there in all that cold he looked suddenly like a grinning snowman. I started to laugh so hard I became hysterical.

Somehow he managed to haul sobbing me and that sodden tree all the way back to the car, with me feeling selfish and frightened. For God's sake, what if he died from carrying me? Worse, what if he never loved me?

Back in the car with the engine running and the heater on, he yanked my boots off and rubbed my bare toes hard.

"Sorry," I said, looking at the bent shoulders of his red plaid hunting coat.

"Let's get you some boots on the way home," he said.

And it really happened that way. I got a pair of tall rubber boots just like his. Boots that my mother called a waste of money. Boots she knew I'd grow out of too quickly.

She yelled and yelled but in the end it was useless because she lost something that day, involuntarily surrendering a chunk of a boy's heart to a stranger who had finally learned how to be a dad.

It's a dog's death: Bad day for Buffy the cocker spaniel

March 14, 1993

This is not funny, absolutely and completely not funny.

Buffy died. It's tragic. She had so much to live for, the vile cur.

Let me come clean here. Buffy was a cocker spaniel, and I don't especially like cocker spaniels or any dog smaller than a Cadillac El Dorado. It's a male thing affecting a great number of guys with tattooed necks and me.

Where was I? Oh right, Buffy. Before you go all weepy, you should know that the Buff was 14, that's 98 human years. She can't, of course, recall either world war, Vietnam or even The Beatles' "white album" for all her years. But we should all be so lucky with the little L.L. Bean doggie bed, the nightly smorgasbord (picky eater) and the constant attention from her adoring owners, Fred and Gladys.

Those aren't their real names. I'm just borrowing them from aliases used by Prince Charles and Camilla because my good friends—whose real names are Linda and Bob—didn't want their actual names used and didn't even want me to mention poor dear Buffy in my "stupid column" unless I promised not to make fun of all the weird stuff that happened to the flea-riddled departed.

So don't laugh when I report that, on a recent morning, one of Gladys' daughters woke up, found Buffy lying like a sleepy golden lox on her L.L. Bean doggie bed and yelled, "Mom! I think the Buffster croaked!"

I should mention that Fred and Gladys got Buffy as a sort of try-on for kids. They figured, and this is common reasoning, that if they could handle a dog, they could handle a kid. HA! Show me a kid who can survive in the yard for two days on a large bowl of Alpo and I'll show you the perfect child.

As it turned out, they loved Buffy so much that they had two children, both of whom were intensely hated by the snarling, unpleasant-smelling beast. Naturally, the children weren't terribly upset when they found Buffy dead as a rat in the kitchen. Gladys, on the other hand, was beside herself because Buffy was her first "baby."

It happens all the time. So do frantic calls to vets who are forced to mumble soothing words about bringing the dog in for transport to the next life and, "Yes, yes, it is ever so sad."

And that's exactly what Gladys did, loading the now mortally heavy Buff, wrapped in a tartan travel blanket, on the back seat of her car after crowding her two girls into the right front seat because neither had any more affection for the dog in death than they did in life.

Sad as Gladys was, she had work and school drop-off to think about and, well, the vet's office was right on the way to the freeway.

But don't you know, this would be the morning that a truck would pull directly into their path, causing Gladys to slam on the brakes and the suddenly unshrouded Buffy to come flying up between the two front seats and directly into the dashboard—PLOP!

Gladys looked down at the dead dog and then over at

her older daughter, a plea for help on her stricken face. "I'm not touching it!" the kid said and meant it.

Lacking options, stout Gladys got out of the car in traffic, climbed into the back seat and gave the supine Buffmeister a good yank. It didn't move. She yanked again harder, and again, harder than that. This time the pup pulled free and landed on her lap.

"Will somebody come back here and hold this dead dog?" she asked in her bad-morning mom voice. Nobody would, no way. With some effort—her butt sticking out of the car the whole time—Gladys strapped dead Buffy in with a seat belt, a seat belt she had great difficulty undoing when she got to the vet's office.

This after stopping at the school and hearing her children scream, "Come look at our dead dog!" to the other drop-offs who ran in greatish numbers to see the woman in a business suit with a dead cocker spaniel in the back seat.

"Cool!" one kid said, pressing his nose against the glass. "And he's wearing a seat belt," said another. "Your mom must be really strict."

Later on the phone, Gladys blathered to me about Buff. Ah, yes, Buffy. She hated children, hated everyone, but loved her and loved her husband who wasn't there ("as usual!") to fight that seat belt and help carry the furry baggage into the vet's office to discuss "arrangements" like a scene right out of "Friday The 13th: Part XVI."

She decided on dignified cremation for Buffy. And maybe I shouldn't have said that the ashes will soon be fertilizing banana trees in Central America. After all, the dog bit me only twice—breaking the skin only once. And I hold no grudges, not me.

Hello night, good night old lady

July 13, 1984

It all occurred to me as I sponged my feverish 20-month-old daughter.

Even with an air conditioner aimed at her wet skin, she was 103 degrees.

My wife and I had labored for hours, bathing the crying child in cool water, to get her temperature down from a high of 105 degrees. Now they were asleep, leaving me alone with the humming machine and the living heat rising off the small body into the palm of my hand.

Among the jumble of images that came to me as I sat beside her was a page from one of her storybooks. And that image evoked an incident from a few weeks earlier. Night had fallen while the child, completely absorbed, busied herself with her Lego blocks. Finally looking up from her task, she was startled by the suddenly black sky outside our large rear windows.

"Hello night," she said meekly.

It was one of those exquisite moments when you wonder whether a child will ever be that cute again. The incident stuck in my mind because it somehow made the possibility of losing her more terrifyingly real than usual. I say usual, because the thought of losing her, the possibility that she might not be there, is always—as it is with all parents—in the back of my mind.

In the storybook that triggered this depressing line of thought, a small bunny had just been put to bed. Carrying it further, I guessed that the bunny, in his pajamas, is meant to be my daughter's age. Like her, he has just begun to suspect that the world offers far more fright than solace.

So, one by one, this apprehensive bunny says good night to the things around him.

Stars, moon, chairs, tables, a milk glass, toys, a duck and pictures are all bid good night.

It's all completely unremarkable, actually, unless you happen to be 20 months old and trying to remember the names for all the things around you, or unless you happen to be a grown man up at 2 a.m. with a sick child under your helpless hand.

"Good night old lady who sits in the chair and waits," the bunny says, finally, to an old woman bunny who is well . . . sitting in a rocking chair and doing just that.

She sits and rocks and knits and waits this ancient creature of great love.

And that image brought back the memory of a real old lady who sat and waited and watched.

I was as sick as this child, part of a nation of children smitten by the Asian flu epidemic of 1958.

In a stream of memory that includes school, comic books, church and baseball, stands this small spot of delirium. For two weeks, I was so terribly ill that it stands out like an opium dream, a blur of worried faces and doctors. A blur, except for the old lady who sat and said nothing. The latter was understandable when you consider that she spoke only Italian, not the language of choice for a 7-year-old boy trying to be as American as Joe DiMaggio.

But she came and stayed.

While others fretted, she would touch my forehead

and say her rosary, mixing the old words of Christian prayer with even more ancient words. Passed from women to women and only on All Souls Eve, the words were said to dispel fevers and disease, the like of which killed seven of her eight children before they were a year old.

Stout and heavily lined, in my young mind my grandmother was like something made of stone.

I recall looking at her during those long days, thinking that nothing could penetrate the wall of mystery she quietly built around us after the men of science left. It was a silent bond between us, passed to her along an unbroken chain of women that extended back to the dark times in the land of misery she left behind.

I couldn't mumble the words and, sadly, I lack the armor she wore against the world's terrible changes.

But, tired as I was, I could sit and wait and know that I could repay at least a little of the ancient debt that binds us.

Visit to Dachau camp can leave one alone—and afraid

April 21, 1985

Forty years after liberation, the terrible image of the Nazi death camps is still powerful enough to ensnare a president and remind us that what is past is always potentially prologue.

I have been to Dachau. I went with my head down, wondering at my own motives and half-expecting my request for directions to be scorned. Instead, I found people on the streets of Munich willing to direct me there like it was a local beer hall. Still, the presence of the camp, though partially financed by the Bavarian government, is not a well-publicized fact.

Tourist offices carry no information on the former munitions-plant-turned-work camp that lies just beyond their city limits.

It has been a few years, but I can recall the subway ride through prosperous suburbs and the sign over one old station house that read "Dachau."

Like me, many people have stood on its platform—as they have since the camp was reopened in 1965—wondering why there are no posted directions. Finally aboard a connector bus, passengers spoke in low tones, most looked embarrassed.

"Camp!" the driver mumbled, bored.

Outside, I fixed on the tan-and-brown watchtowers that rise from the high walls and barbed wirelike darkened lighthouses.

"Visit Dachau's 1,200-year-old artist's center," reads a sign opposite the entrance, reminding us that Bavaria existed long before Hitler.

It also was making a last effort to kill in us the coward that didn't want to enter.

Inside, the barren vastness of the exercise yard allied with the wind to make me look over my shoulder toward the open highway.

In the administration building, in rooms where people were murdered, hangs an objective view of the Third Reich's rise to power and what is now known officially as Memorial Site Concentration Camp Dachau.

It was as though it had all happened in another country, or on another planet.

Murals depicting the workings of the massive camp system are displayed along with photographs of camp life beginning in March 1933, two months after Hitler's rise to power.

On these grounds were shot, worked to death, experimented upon, starved, hung, and tortured to death 31,951 people out of the 206,000 prisoners registered here.

Gathered from throughout Germany, they were political opponents of the Reich, Jews, clergy and other "undesirables."

You can see them, broken and starving in the German and allied footage shown in the film theater. Just outside is a souvenir shop selling postcard pictures of the camp ovens.

I can remember the crunching sound of my shoes on the gravel as I passed the single reconstructed barrack, the live wire, ditch and tower on the way to the "krematorium." It stands in a beautifully tended garden where

6,000 Russian POWs were shot. Inside the same bleak structure is a gas chamber, installed but never used. Dachau prisoners marked for death were sent to the Harthiem Castle near Linz, Austria.

The ovens, with gray dust and fresh flowers at their mouths, were the main attraction. Only small children spoke while adults aimed cameras into the surprisingly innocuous-looking structure.

It was strange how absolutely practical the camp looked. In its current state, it could well be any state prison or a nearly deserted movie set. That is, a set with the ability to make itself unforgettable.

A German friend later struck a nerve when he said that many nations must take part of the responsibility for Dachau.

"It is a hideous memory," he said. "Keeping it alive may be a form of self-punishment, a perversion badly needed to remind us, never again."

Those dark words are inscribed on the black, steel sculpture—a grotesque standing rectangle whose individual pieces are shaped like body parts—that stands near shrines representing the Jewish and Christian faiths.

But what I saw there didn't fully strike me until three days later.

Stranded at an Autobahn rest stop, I stood watching trucks pass, their lights cutting the mist and illuminating a line of hitchikers standing nearby.

In the darkness they were anonymous, semi-human forms. Hands thrust deep in pockets made their movements zombie-like.

As I watched this sunken-eyed crowd a nightmarish feeling filled me. I was yanked loose from reality and for that moment unable to tell who they were or who I was.

I was suddenly alone in this alien place and afraid.

Looking out on the Spey, a Scotsgirl cycle is complete

June 17, 1985

I have a picture of a young girl standing outside the Gordon Arms Hotel in the Scottish Highland village of Tomintoul. She is wearing a ridiculously bright party dress, a real swinging London number if there ever was one, and posing beside a red Triumph motor car.

In truth, the girl was faking it, trying to look like an adult preparing to drive stylishly away from this century-old hotel in a wild and remote area 150 miles north of Edinburgh.

That Scotsgirl is now a business executive, a mother and my wife. And I tell this story only because I recently returned to the Gordon Arms with her and found myself half expecting to find that same car parked on the green.

There's a joke that applies here.

How many Scots does it take to change a light bulb?

Three: one to change the bulb and two to stand around saying, "Shame to see such a wonderful old light bulb go."

While the rest of Europe drives madly toward an uncertain future, parts of Scotland appear to be, if not set in amber, at least delightfully stuck in it.

The stuff of tourism aside—bagpipes, kilts and other postcard fantasies—there is a sense of timelessness about this place.

It had been well over a decade since my wife made her last visit to the venerable old pile with her parents and it was as if she had left yesterday.

A few weeks ago we stepped into the lobby out of a stiff wind and ran straight into the woman who has been cleaning the hotel for decades.

Without missing a beat, the Highlander looked at my wife and said, "Well, Margot, I trust you won't be making a mess this time?"

The mess in question involved a carpet, Margot, her sister, two girlfriends and a couple of dozen buttered scones that been stuffed down their shirt-fronts for a clandestine midnight snack.

The same Oriental carpet that had absorbed the butter from the fumbled scones all those years ago still lines the old, dark stairs. The rooms, too, are unchanged. Even the 90-year-old mystery bullet hole in a front window is a revered part of the decor.

The hotel is owned by the Grant family, which isn't surprising when almost everybody in the region is a Grant.

Even the nearest town is called Grantown on Spey, the Spey being the river that supplies much of the water to the local whiskey distilleries.

A Grant daughter was serving drinks on our first night there. As locals sat around singing to accordion music, she asked my wife if she remembered their last conversation.

"Of course I do," Margot replied, recalling the day when—on one of the family's many visits—she remarked that she was sick of heather. "You told me, 'Insult the heather and you insult Scotland.'"

It goes further than that. Insult old hotels, with worn-smooth furniture, bathrooms across the hall and those ceramic hot-water bottles in the bed, and you insult a way of life.

Although I am intimate with this land, each visit requires a transition period for what at first seems merely old to take on the glow of polished brass.

Within days my city paranoia leaves and our room remains unlocked while we walk green and deserted hills.

If man has a natural state, this, for me, is it.

At this latitude, well north of Moscow, it doesn't get dark until 11 p.m. this time of year. On one long evening I stood with my small daughter looking down on this portion of her mother's native land.

While she counted "One sheeps, two sheeps, five sheeps," I could see Tomintoul in the distance, with its three streets and its squat, stone cottages. On the Spey, a fisherman was casting in the shallows while his gillie, dressed in tweed plus fours, reclined on the bank.

Within my sweeping field of vision were slate-roofed farmhouses, rabbits, a stag and two black-and-white collies quietly moving a flock of sheep and new lambs across a pasture. One great Victorian house stood resolutely on a hillside.

Its perfection struck me. This was exactly the kind of rural valley I'd seen in geography books when I was a child.

Beside me a little girl in red rubber boots stood on ground where her mother had played long years ago.

Below us the vast theater stretched. I could almost see those big geography book arrows rising from Earth to sky and back again illustrating life's great cycles. And for this one moment, the circle was complete.

Selling a house is easy—just open a vein

August 11, 1985

I just sold my house. That sounds simple enough on the surface. However, upon deeper examination (and I think I'm ready for one), it is a lot like saying, "I just had my brain removed."

Of course, such a statement suggests I still have a brain.

"What are you complaining about? It's over," you sunny optimists say.

To this I reply: When you are selling a house, it's never over.

You see, what I actually have after many weeks in the housing wars is an "offer." That is real estate talk. It means that someone has agreed to buy the place if they can get the money.

I, on the other hand, have made my own offer on another house using the nonexistent "money" from this "sold" house as a phantom down payment.

The escrow (from an old French word for big trouble) for both houses are supposed to close simultaneously.

Positioned at the bottom of this house of cards is the escrow company, complete strangers who are supposedly killing themselves at this very moment to make the deal work.

But all this is beside the point. It is the selling of the house that I am concerned with, a home that I very much like.

Still, when contemplating its sale, I did not adopt the old my-home-is-the-best-in-the-universe attitude that real estate agents so hate.

No, we studied the market. We made comparisons and we took notes.

What we had was a not-too-small house with charm. Charm is a real estate agent word.

I didn't know that my house had charm. Neither did many of the would-be buyers who somehow just saw it as just another piece of overpriced (Note from present: at $125,000 can you believe?) termite food.

At first, the great number of them walking across our freshly waxed floors made me think we had an easily saleable item.

Then I started listening to the sales pitch: "This is the stove. This is the door. And look, a window."

I don't mean to represent all these hard-working, would-be collectors of 6 percent commissions as lame staters of the obvious. I'm just saying that several of them certainly seemed to be, well, lame.

"How thick are these wood floors?" one asked, ignoring unimportant items like pipes and roofing. From that moment, I tried to avoid the nightmarish strangers wandering around my house talking like theater critics.

"The family room is tremendous in scope. Not since Elm Street have I seen such a flawed poetic vision. Too bad the tile is broken while this particular shade of poison-pen blue is an abomination before God."

As I washed dishes one evening, an agent and her clients walked unannounced into my kitchen and set to work inspecting the interior of the refrigerator before turning their attention to a painting.

"Korean art, very beautiful," the gentleman said.

"It's Japanese," I replied.

"No, it's Korean," he replied. "I'm Korean. I know."

I showed him the artist's signature.

"Maybe it's not so nice after all," he grumbled and left.

That, however, was not the encounter that broke me. When I think of it, the strain had been mounting for weeks. Aside from thoughts of ruinous swing loans, the worst of it was the constant cleaning and maintaining of the place in the Home Beautiful mode.

On top of that, we had to forgo dinners, breakfasts, lunches and naps for the sake of a quick sale that never materialized. It was into this climate that they wandered.

There was a large woman, a tiny man and a midsize agent. They spent an hour inspecting the place in detail: closets, cupboards—the whole rotten shot.

Meanwhile, small daughter, wife and I sat on the patio pretending that we were really enjoying reading "If You Give a Mouse a Cookie" for the 11,000th time.

"Nice antiques," the big woman said through the screen door.

"The antiques aren't for sale," I said, forcing a smile.

"Oh, I know that," she replied airily, "but that's why we came. Our friend here said you had nice antiques."

My wife shot me a hard glance. At this point, she knew her husband was capable of terrorist statements and violent acts.

Actually, I don't know why I should have been angry. So what if I had given up my privacy. And it was certainly beneath me to be angry because a small army of agents could not do what a neighbor did in two weeks with a $2 "For Sale by Owner" sign.

She was right. I was about to become a headline—"Reporter assaults lookie-loo"—when the child (Note from future: the child is now 25 and pretty much the same) piped in.

"Go away," she said, with a 3-year-old's cold resolution. "And don't go in my room."

I gave her a tough-guy look for appearance's sake, but in my heart of hearts, I knew she was my own lifeblood.

A look back at letting go for the first time

September 10, 1985

It's all way down the road, real life, real school.

This was still play school, preschool, I told myself, as my 3-year-old daughter and I walked hand-in-hand into her new day-care center.

Separation was not new to us. Like half the parents in the United States, we've been sending Caitlin to a sitter since she was 6 months old. We'd reconciled ourselves to a two-career life, which is not to say it was easy in the early days.

It took time. But it soon became clear that she was developing normally.

What am I saying? She was thriving and she loved her sitter, Ann McKinnon.

I learned this last fact one cold morning a little more than a year ago.

Waking up ill, she demanded, "I want mommy." Great, there I was alone while mommy was 3,000 miles away in New York on business.

Women, I told myself, had been silently coping with exactly this kind of situation for centuries. Suddenly, here I was, a man facing down a childhood illness (by the way, all childhood illnesses at first appear fatal to me) alone and I seemed to be losing.

"Mommy is in New York," I told her soothingly.

She sat up, stared at me through watery eyes and proclaimed, "OK, then Ann." Even children know the natural order in these situations.

As her third birthday approached, the waiting list at the difficult-to-get-into Child Educational Center finally yielded Caitlin a space. Ann knew it was time. We knew it was time, but it wasn't easy. We all had familial memories.

There was the time Caitlin—born with opinions on matters of taste—had helped the sitter pick a wardrobe for a European cruise. It went like this:

"Do you like this dress?" Ann would ask.

The kid would regard it seriously for a moment, her outsized brown eyes taking on the look of a rag-trader. "Yuk," she'd offer disdainfully, or "Gorgeous." Her first big word.

On Friday we said our goodbyes. And although Ann had done her best to prepare the child for entry into the larger day-care world, she walked away happily proclaiming, "Ann will be at the new school, too."

Saturday was parents day and I might have felt differently were the new school not located in a real elementary school building.

From a home environment, Caitlin would join the Dolphin class in a room full of toys and 3-year-olds watched over by no less than three cheery teachers.

Ann's house was just that, a house, a home. This new place has a playground, freedom to run and a philosophy. Responsibility, sharing, numbers and letters would subtly enter Caitlin's young mind through it.

There also would be group songs, stories, a nap, lunch, snacks, playtime and many ongoing life demonstrations.

Plants grew from seeds in the classroom, hamsters grew from whatever it is that baby hamsters are called and the single goldfish in a bowl would soon become a frog.

A little boy named Ben told me that as his father and I helped clean the room for Monday's class start.

Within minutes Saturday, Caitlin was playing while the adults engaged in the subtle yuppie sport of trying to out-parent each other.

"We believe that little Nigel should have all the space he needs."

Some people actually said things like that.

As I worked, I watched her play—so confident, so interested in all the new gadgets.

There had not been a great deal of outward change in my life in the three years since she was born. I am still 6 feet tall, still working at the same job, living in the same house and even driving the same car.

For Caitlin, during that same time, a world has come to pass. I thought of her birth and how, in retrospect, her determined little personality seemed to come into the world with her. We'd even come to think that it was there as she kicked her poor mother senseless from the inside.

I remembered the long nights with her 8-pound body on my chest, rising and falling with my breath. And I remember the shock of realizing how tentative her young life was, how close it seemed to its creator. I feared that she would somehow slip away.

How odd. Moments after the birth of this stranger, I knew I didn't want to live without her.

I didn't ever want her to leave.

As I watched her play Saturday, I knew that this was still true. The risk had been taken.

I'd given over completely. Yet I knew that by bits and pieces, the leaving had already begun.

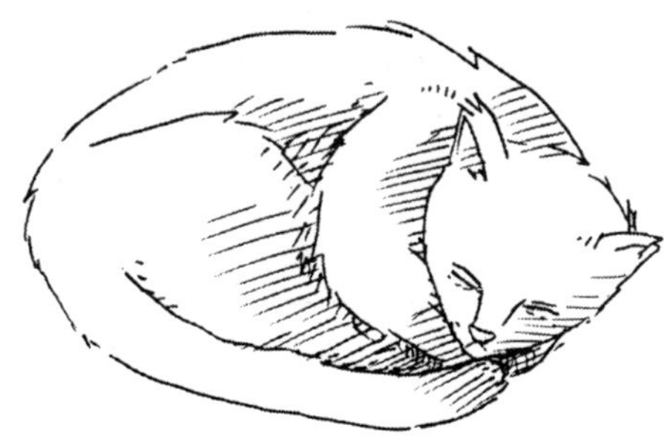

Cat's death teaches youngster the meaning of purr-manence

December 2, 1985

Our cat Dave died last week, leaving a noticeable hole in the fabric of our small family.

It probably seems silly to go on about a 6-pound gray cat while so many humans are suffering in this world.

Still, it is difficult to forget a creature that lived with us for seven years after we found him nearly dead from dehydration by our back fence.

Actually, he was on the other side of our back fence on a killingly hot July day. I had just returned from a Saturday assignment to find my wife and our house guest, David Cameron, wandering around the garden looking up at the trees.

"There's an injured bird somewhere," David said, directing my attention upward. Now I'm not exactly Grizzly Adams when it comes to nature, but I could tell that the noise wasn't coming from a bird.

The highly vexed "mew, mew, mew" cutting through the dead-hot air was definitely being made by a cat. And that cat was over by the fence, not up in a tree.

"Here's your bird," I said after locating the tiny kitten.

"Get him," my wife directed.

"He's on the other side of the fence. This is someone else's cat," I replied, realizing where we were heading.

"He's dying," she said, making it clear that it was going to be either divorce court or the cat.

I pulled the boards far enough apart for her to reach in and yank the animal into the world of the living for the second time in his short life.

He looked awful.

"He won't make it," I announced as the cat lapped up an entire saucer of milk. Then, "On the other hand, maybe he will."

Finding an appropriate name was simple. As the cat sucked up a second helping of milk, we went through the possibilities. Big Ears, Scrawny, Insufferable and Probably Stupid came to mind.

We then looked up at our tall and scrawny friend, Dave who was talking on the phone.

"Dave," we said, pleasing Dave, the tall and scrawny human.

And so Dave the cat wormed his way into our lives—after my neighbor denied ever seeing the beast.

Years later we would tell our small daughter that Dave was our first child. We were joking, but attending to his cat illnesses and his inconvenient needs did help prepare us for the disruptions of child rearing.

When he died last Sunday of a fast-working feline ailment, I realized how completely his life was intertwined with our own.

In retrospect, I'd say that Dave's greatest asset was his ability to just be there. It didn't matter how long you worked at the typewriter or in the garden, he'd just stay right there.

He was great company.

Eventually, our daughter started applying her newly

found verbal skills to him.

"Come here, Dave!" she'd demand, pointing to her feet. Mostly, he would exercise the age-old cat right to ignore any and all commands. Yet sometimes he would come and bump a soft gray flank against her stubby little legs, making her laugh.

I remember her dismay when she tried this same command on a dog and got knocked down for her trouble.

Dave became a living lesson for her as she grew older. He had to be fed, groomed, scolded and brought to the doctor, as did she.

Through him she also learned something about gentleness, a trait that doesn't come as standard equipment on children.

Then he died.

The books (and if this isn't a reason to avoid parenting books I don't know what is) tell me that such losses prepare children for bigger deaths. It's supposed to work like this: "Dave died, mom and dad will die, other children will die, and someday I, too, will pass."

We talked and explained like the unconvinced, first-time parental idiots that we are, but the question of Dave's whereabouts seemed far from settled in the 3-year-old's mind.

"Dave is buried. He's not coming back, right?" she asked for about the 50th time last night, breaking my heart for the 50th time.

When I told her that she was correct, she thought for a moment, then added:

"OK, then we'll get another little gray cat and we'll call him Dave. . . . But it won't be the real Dave, will it?"

So a rotten, terrible, awful and probably uncalled for lesson had been learned from a most unlikely but very worthy source.

Glowing holiday memories emblazoned in neon lights

December 25, 1985

It was the Baci candy that did it. A friend passed the chocolate bon-bons around at a party. Made by the confectioner Perugina in Perugia, Italy, they come foil-wrapped and memory-laden.

Neon memories to be exact, of a near-penniless Christmas spent in Rome a decade ago.

I've always maintained that there are only two ways to travel: With a lot of money or with almost none at all. In the first instance, you can buy anything you want. In the second, if you are young, good people just might take pity on you.

Dinners and beds are given without thought of repayment.

In our case, the bottom floor of a two-floor penthouse near the Coliseum was supplied my wife and me by the mother of a close high school pal who had married an

Italian and moved to the Eternal City.

It was meant to be a short visit, but my very young wife and I seemed to strike a chord in the older couple who were without their own grown children for the first time in many years.

In my memory, the fall and winter months we spent with them are tinted a deep terra cotta.

The bright tourist summer had vanished with the cold. Rain dripped from bare trees and penetrated ancient stones.

The bleakness suited us that year. Our international marriage had not thrilled our parents. And although we were educated to the usual extent, we had no jobs and no prospects in a world overrun with people exactly like us.

In fact, all we really had was love and the decrepit Austin Mini van, bought from a shepherd for 90 pounds. that had taken us from my wife's home in Britain to this huge city.

There was no plan. We were just hiding out, covering our lack of direction with a tourist guise.

Each day we'd spend hours walking the city. In time we came to know its cheapest and best restaurants, its poorer quarters and its ancient secret places.

In the Vatican we found the grave of Scotland's Bonnie Prince Charles, the pretender to the British crown. Crushed by the English in battle, he went to Rome and died in lonely exile. And here he rests behind eternally closed doors guarded by two stricken angels, a Catholic and a king who knew his country only briefly.

We saw the room where young Keats died and the foreign cemetery that held his remains and all that was left of countless less-famous dreamers not unlike ourselves. It is a city that always has tolerated fops and fools and survived to accommodate them in 1,000 layers of decay. And it tolerated us, our highs and lows and our confusion as we walked its streets with something approaching a sense of purpose.

In time we started acting like Italians, eating endless lunches and dinners, taking siestas and hanging out.

Then there would be moments of crushing homesickness for the English language, a hunger that could be mitigated only by crossing the raging winter Tiber to attend the city's single English-language cinema. It is odd to walk in a cold wind across 1,000-year-old bridges to drink warm Cokes, to eat things that resembled hotdogs and to watch images of cowboys in a Western desert that neither of us had yet seen. Anything was good, as long as it was in English.

That single theater became a refuge within a refuge, from life and from the giant Fellini movie that played out 24 hours a day in the streets.

Family arguments, buses that wouldn't stop for passengers, cars that wouldn't stop for pedestrians, water that stopped in midshower and people looking over your shoulder in the bank, these were only part of the general Roman hassle.

Still, no matter how sordid it got, it looked good to two young people with no real place of their own. It is odd now to think we should have felt this way as Christmas approached and the ancient piazzas filled with Italians hawking wares and selling chestnuts roasted on small charcoal fires.

Maybe we would have hung out there forever, eventually dying of that peculiar Roman torpor that affects some foreigners. Then came a freezing winter snowstorm that struck while we sat snug in our movie theater.

We emerged into the night, ill-dressed for the deluge and headed through twisting streets in what we thought was the general direction of our borrowed home. It wasn't, and we soon knew that we were lost and seriously cold.

Wasn't this a fine mess, freezing to death on a Roman street corner?

"OK, how about some light!" I yelled at the snowy heavens. It broke the tension. My wife laughed, so did several passersby, who probably had no idea what I was saying.

That's when I saw the light penetrating all that snow and blackness, standing huge and blue in the Western sky. It was the direction of home, it was the direction of our future.

Its neon said "BACI."

That's Italian for "KISS."

So it wasn't a burning bush. In this world you have to take your signs the way they come.

Space shuttle's failed mission united Americans in sorrow

January 28, 1986

It was years ago, in a foreign place, when a man said to me: "You Americans expect to be the first on the moon, don't you. You just expect to be the first to do everything, to go into space, to photograph Mars? The universe is yours, isn't it?"

After a moment's thought, I had to admit that most of us did expect to be there—wherever there was—first, although it was probably not something we sat around thinking about. The expectation was just there, in our national character. We expect to field the best team, the hottest rockets.

We expect to put schoolteachers and journalists into space while some nations struggle just to feed themselves. And sometimes, like when Challenger exploded in the midst of its incredible run skyward this morning, we pay the price.

Maybe it would have been easier to see all that harnessed fury cut so horribly loose over the Gulf Stream if we had expected it. But there has been nothing in our space program to prepare us for this.

Russians, sure. They lost people in flight. But somehow, fairly or not, we expect that of them. We had losses, paying our dues years ago when three astronauts burned in their capsule as it sat atop a rocket that was still bolted to the ground. But this was supposed to be different. The shuttle was so routine, so elegant, so beautifully predictable we could send congressmen, schoolteachers and reporters up like they were taking a 747 to Atlanta.

Somehow, and I don't know how, we came to ignore that 700-foot-long cone of fire shooting out of the back of those solid rockets. Somehow we forgot all that oxygen and hydrogen, a half-million gallons of it.

We didn't connect hydrogen gas with the Hindenburg collapsing in flames all those long years ago, with our atavistic fear of fire, with our quiet, but still-lingering distrust of flight. We became blase despite what our eyes told us. Awesome power and technology had been reduced to pictures of weightless astronauts chasing Jell-O across the crew cabin.

It wasn't even like the old days when there were just a few astronaut heroes to occupy our attention. There had come to be so many mission specialists and fliers of this great dead-stick machine that we failed to note their names except when one turned out to be a woman or, in the case of the Challenger's last mission, a mother and a schoolteacher from Concord, N.H.

"Roger, go with throttle up," and it was over, sweet dreams and flying machines in pieces . . . Nothing left but a column of white smoke in a matchless blue sky to mark where seven people and an orbiter flew seconds before.

As I write this, the networks are rerunning that explosive moment over and over as if, having seen it once, our memories will ever again need refreshing.

The ability to speak leaves us and we realize how we are bound together. In this building and in offices along this street, in schools, wherever there is a television, people are watching. If you are alone, you probably felt a need to call someone, anyone.

We've seen it before, years ago when a president died, when the three astronauts burned. Suddenly, we realize what we are and who we are and it has nothing to do with cheap patriotism. It is deeper than that. We expect to see a fine young teacher from old Concord existing inside such coldly beautiful technology. We expect to have the hottest rocket . . . we expect to be number one.

Then comes the horror 23 miles up, and we are reminded of adventure's downside: tragedy, mortality and terrible waste. Think of the families, consider the motherless children and the children everywhere who saw the tragic end of human beings at their peak moment, of man at his very best aboard a failed rocket.

Now we are not so blase as we were only this morning. We know what test pilot Chuck Yeager was talking about when he mentioned that tank of fuel, an explosion waiting to happen, sitting behind him in a test aircraft. And we again know about suffering together as a people.

Comet watch produces a street light and a warm glow

March 23, 1986

You'll have to excuse me.

I'm red-eyed and tired, and I swear it has nothing to do with booze. It's that comet. Actually, it's the kid and the comet . . . and me.

You see, I had this idea that the 3- year-old should see the thing on Friday morning, one of the last good days for viewing the potato-shaped, hurtling heavenly body.

By today, it would have been obscured by the moon and Saturday was out because I had planned to sleep until the kid wakes us up or 7 a.m. So there we stood on the front porch in the predawn, bundled up and scanning the lower portion of the southern horizon with binoculars.

"What do you see?" she asked, hanging on to my right leg with both arms.

"A street light," I answered.

"Let me see," she asked, and I handed her the optical device that she calls "nokalers."

"It's beautiful!" she enthused.

"What is?"

"The street light," she said, pulling away. "You can have a turn when I'm finished."

With that, she began to scan the street, the big (what

she calls) "nokalers" cradled in her rather large (for a 3-year-old) hands.

Something told me that the Bogert/ Halley expedition was already a bust.

If I had been like my own father, I would have fired up an unfiltered Camel with my Zippo and sat down. Lacking the habit or the inclination for a suffocating death, I just sat down and let the small, parka-clad figure lean against me.

"Try looking at the sky for the comet," I said, tilting the glasses upward for her. She did, but the way she pulled the nokalers away again told me that this was—as usual—her show.

"You know, Caitlin, that comet only comes around once in a great, great while."

No answer, but the glasses bobbed up and down a fraction as she continued viewing the empty southern sky.

"When it comes back this way again you'll be very old and I won't be here," I added, suddenly wishing I hadn't interjected such a somber thought into our morning muse.

"That's OK, daddy, I'll remember you," she replied, without a hint of emotion, the bottoms of the eyepieces still pressing into her fat cheeks.

That's a deal we made. I'd be a decent father and, in return, she'd remember me when the occasion called for it. Like when Halley's Comet returned, for example.

As it turns out, the somber thought was somber only for me. She'd made that deal without fully understanding it. What am I saying. I don't fully understand it myself. I know only that life keeps chugging along, changing me as it goes. First there was me the single guy, then me with a wife, then me with a kid. With each of those steps, I couldn't remember what the previous life was like.

That's how I came to stand out there on the cold steps at 5 a.m. with a 3-year-old. Plus, this is the least of what

I have done and, to my own amazement, done gladly.

And I'm not talking about the late-night walkabouts when she was an infant. I'm talking about the increasingly silly things I find myself doing.

Take last Christmas, when the two of us went shopping for her mother's presents.

Imagine what I looked like to the edgy saleswoman who stood watching me from her side of the counter (where she could not see the child at my side) apparently arguing with myself over the perfume display.

Then there are Saturdays at the L.A Athletic Club, where we take her to dance and swim. Think of me at her first dancing lesson, haggling with another child's mother over a pair of tap shoes her daughter had just out grown. She wanted ten. I offered five. We compromised on seven.

And have you ever tried to get a female into dancing tights. It's just not something guys are trained for.

I've also put her headband on, tied her tap shoes and waited outside the door while she and her dance mates clattered through a routine while singing in high-pitched, glass-shattering little-girl voices, "We are the sunshine dancing kids, watch us shine."

Then comes the swim lesson. I'm the swim teacher, so of course I wait for her and her mother to exit the women's locker room.

I used to come here to do manly things, like exercising. I recall as I stand on the steps of the kids' pool, holding a pink rubber life ring.

In the pool and outside waiting for the comet, I wonder at how impervious to cold she seems.

"Wait!" she exclaimed, disappearing into the house. When she emerged into the half-light of dawn she was carrying the nokalers and her View Master.

"Here, now you have your own," she said, handing me the red plastic toy.

What could I do but sit there beside her, scanning the

horizon for a comet (which we never did see) through a faint View Master image of Donald Duck and a warm glow that I hope will be remembered.

Prenatal program for older moms: needles and family trees

April 25, 1986

My wife and I went in for something called prenatal diagnosis.

Through all human history, people were happy just to produce live children. So they had lots of them, a fact that is evidenced by today's high property values.

These days, if you are past the age of 30 and pregnant, the first thing people say isn't "Congratulations," it's "Are you going to have amniocentesis?"

This trend is, I'm sure, exaggerated in my mind because everybody I know is over 30 and having babies and, well, it's like anything else. If the technology is there, we use it.

Besides, this amniocentesis keeps an awful lot of doctors busy who might otherwise be getting into trouble on street corners.

I will not make light of amniocentesis itself, the process by which amniotic fluid is drawn out of a pregnant woman's uterus through a hollow needle inserted into the abdominal wall, then tested for genetic disorders.

That's because there is nothing even remotely funny about a test which, if the medical community hadn't convinced us otherwise, would sound like some 14th century torture.

It is easy for me to say that the brief, relatively painless and utterly terrifying procedure went off without a hitch, because I wasn't the one lying on the table.

Because of local anesthetic and the obvious skill of a doctor, there was, my wife reports, little pain except that generated by the thought of having the chamber where a living fetus lies violated by a sharp metal object.

I say living because no life could be more certain than that which flashed around on the video screen of the ultrasound (sonograph) machine that showed the doctor where the baby was.

"There are the two lobes of its brain," the doctor said, like he was describing something that might come on a Chevy. At that moment, the sound waves passing through the sonograph's hand-held wand penetrated the soft skull of the ever-moving fetus.

It turned this way and that, face, big eyes, huge mouth, feet, the image was like a photo negative, like the image on the Shroud of Turin only a female I guessed because I seem fated to spend my life surrounded by females.

At the moment she was an amphibian, master of her watery world, and it kindled in me an added sense of fatherhood. I could see what my ancestors could only dream of seeing and I accepted what I saw as mine and as something that I was about to love.

The genetic counseling was a different matter.

This part of the diagnostic process, during which a doctor attempted to detect genetic disorders through our family histories, turned out to be a great tension breaker. The doctor, a patient and highly skilled woman who could draw the straight lines of a family tree without a ruler, asked us about our families and with every question we'd smile.

All this mirth when we knew one of us was about to

be stuck with a large needle. When we got past the serious stuff of birth defects, we got down to the question of sanity, a subject that begs for a great deal of latitude and interpretation.

For starters, on my side are my four aunts, all of whom—despite their advanced years—still fight constantly about who is the prettiest. At the moment they are all angry with my Aunt Mary who, well into her 70s, has taken up professional modeling. They had laughed at her until she started getting jobs modeling senior citizen fashions and getting paid for it.

Then there is my parachuting, animal-loving, career-Army sister. And who can forget my grandmother who was famous for consuming vast quantities of food and rising in the night to count the money she kept hidden beneath the rug.

And this is just the beginning. On my wife's side we have an entire line of ancestors stretched up and down the length of Scotland. First and foremost is great-grandfather Donald, the RAF wing commander, who, after retirement, busied himself digging completely useless ditches on his farm.

Then there were the two well-to-do maiden aunts who married a pair of ploughmen, gentle old chaps who scandalized the family by buttering scones at the dinner table and handing them around with their big, rough ploughmen hands.

And who could forget the strange uncle whose hobby was collecting truncheons?

Then there was old Granny Inkster, recently departed, who terrorized everyone with insults so cunning as to make herself a local legend.

Laying it all out on paper like that made it suddenly clear that we do indeed come from people who operated nearly within the bounds of what we call sanity.

Strange to think that the little figure, this as yet unformed little girl, visible on the sonograph screen bears their many genetic fragments. And how could we love this one without loving all the rest?

Child's logic the magical touch that can pull a cat from a hat

October 2, 1986

"Hey Rocky, watch me pull a rabbit out of my hat."

"Roarrrrrrr!"

Cartoon Bullwinkle, for about the billionth time, had found a lion in his top hat.

"Hey, Caitlin, did you see that on TV? Hey, Caitlin, look at this. Pretty funny, huh? That Rocky and Bullwinkle are a pair of cutups."

"Can he pull a cat out of that hat?" the kid asked, looking up momentarily. She had been tracing with paper and pencil on an empty Lee's Macaroon Bar wrapper, down to the words, Fabrique En Ecosse.

"That's French for Made in Scotland," I said, trying to cheer her up with a bit of data.

"Daddy, can't you see that I'm grumpy?"

That was the problem. Rocky, Bullwinkle, Boris, Natasha, nothing has cheered her up completely since black Angus—the cat of nine lives, almost no brains and a $200 artificial hip—disappeared.

There were scant clues. A thunderstorm swept in last week. Then it left, carrying, it seemed, one of the best mousers (a euphemism applied to cats that routinely rip rats limb from limb) man has ever had the semi-fortune of knowing.

"Maybe the lightning got him," she said, having turned her attention to dressing a My Little Pony.

"I know how much of, but not of what," Bullwinkle was saying on television.

"Look at that. Old Bullwinkle accidentally made the world's most powerful rocket fuel from a cake recipe."

"Uh-huh," she said, casting a melancholy look at me with her huge brown eyes.

That was it. This called for another search party. Search parties always cheered her up. Or, at least, they offered hope.

We've had a string of bad cat luck these last two years and the kid has been upset by it.

I realize that the shock of losing Dave—her treasured gray cat—to kidney failure last November and the loss of fluffy Sophie to a car the year before is not exactly like exposing your kid to life in the streets of Beirut.

Still, for your average semi-pampered 4-year-old, these were big events. Now, the black, gimpy-hipped panther had vanished and she wanted him back. After all, there was something of a special relationship there.

When he descended from whatever foggy mental mists he lived in, Angus would rub against the kid—and only the kid—begging for a pet. And she'd give him one, saying things like, "Did you wash your face? You're black."

It went right over his head.

So we walked. It was cloudy and cool. She asked: "Where is the sun? Is it going to rain? Is it going to snow? Will there be an earthquake? When is my birthday? When is Christmas?" and would the newly acquired stuffed bear, Teddy Ruxpin, possibly cause Santa to look upon her with a jaundiced eye?

I answered: "Behind the clouds. No. No. Someday. October 18. December 25. Don't worry about Santa. He doesn't care if you have a Teddy Ruxpin. It saves him

$50."

As we walked, we observed our environment. It's amazing what someone 39 inches tall can see.

"Why don't they clean up their yard?" she asked loudly, as she peered through a neighbor's hedge.

We stopped at a garage sale on the next street where we looked through a stack of old phonograph records.

"So where do you think Angus is?" she asked, as I thumbed through the pile.

"Don't know. Look at this, Les Paul and Mary Ford on a 78."

"Maybe he went to Chicago dressed up," she volunteered, in the completely out-of-nowhere manner that has been making me laugh lately.

"Or maybe he went to a restaurant and stayed," she added. "Or maybe the coydoties (a fairly decent try at coyotes) ate him or maybe he moved."

"Without leaving word?" I asked.

"Angus doesn't have words," she said finally.

Back on our own front steps, I was asked to tell The Angus Story, a story about the night her very weird cat died for the very first time. Out there in all the dark and cold outside our tiny house I found him. Then I told her about how, after we sadly wrapped his obviously car-struck body, we buried him in the back yard only to find ourselves being observed by a very much (and quite impossibly) alive Angus.

The sight of his own burial—helped along by the anesthetic administered when his hip was replaced after he actually was hit by a car shortly thereafter—is what we assumed sent Angus into the next room, mentally speaking.

To the betterment of the neighborhood, his misfortunes somehow turned him to full-scale rat genocide and gave rise to belief that Angus, operating in invisible hyperdrive, might live forever.

Then came the lightning and he was gone. We knew he was gone because his dinner went uneaten—a bad sign.

“Well, do you think he’ll come back?” she asked.

“Let’s put it this way,” I said. “I won’t believe he’s really finished until I see a body.”

“Or until he pulls himself out of a hat,” she laughed.

At least she was laughing.

A New York City boy tells how Los Angeles got its name

April 19, 1988

"How are things in Lost Angelus?" my mother asked within scant minutes of my arrival at her Florida home.

No, she did not innocently mispronounce Los Angeles, nor did she mispronounce the name to be merely humorous. No, my mother likes to bring me down a notch or two just so I'll fit into my old bedroom. And she brought up "Lost Angelus" to remind me of a humiliating moment in my early education.

"Ha, ha, Lost Angelus," the casually assembled family laughed.

"What's the joke?" my wife asked.

"The joke is this ..." dear mom began. Then she told the story.

Of course, she had it all wrong. So, in the interest of accuracy, I will tell the story exactly as it happened in my third-grade classroom. Since this isn't a mystery, I'll begin by saying that I knew Lost Angelus was supposed to be Los Angeles but I had to bend a few facts with literary license the size of a framing hammer.

This was the year that, to make sure I didn't start running with boys exactly like me, my parents enrolled me in Catholic school. Being ignorant of the teaching methods employed by nuns—which were, in a few words, "You will learn"—I wasn't actually paying attention during geography.

In truth, I was looking with interest toward the nearby public school grounds where some boys I knew appeared to be bashing each other with baseball bats and I failed to hear the many interesting details about this place called Los Angeles.

I knew the name, honest I did. After all, that's where Walt Disney and Walt Disney's Zorro lived.

Like I said, I just missed a few of the details. You know, things like the city's history and how it related to the lousy, freezing, slummy part of New York State we then called home.

It wasn't until the following Friday afternoon that I learned an important thing about nuns: If they don't catch your errors on the spot, they'll catch you soon enough.

"Take out a sheet of paper and tell me everything you know about Los Angeles," Sister Mary of the Five Holy Wounds directed. This was quickly followed by many happy, twerpy noises from the kiss-up girls who all wanted to be nuns and low grunts from the low boys who all wished they could be out bashing each other with bats. Then we began.

Scratch, scratch, scratch went the pencils, with the kids who actually knew what was going on covering their work with strategically placed elbows. The rest, with the exception of me, soldiered on in true literary fasion.

"Los Angeles, Los Angeles ... Lost Angelus," I said to myself. You see I did take in something about missions and a drawing of little Indian kids praying in front of a cross.

What were they praying for? Could it have anything to do with the mission church's Angelus bell? Could the entire unknown history of the place hinge on this, a lost

Angelus?

My title: “The Lost Angelus.”

Three whole pages I wrote—a page more than the holy-joker girls who I truly wished would all become nuns so they wouldn’t spawn yet more evil female creatures—about the Indian children in this dusty, Zorro-like environment who desperately yearned to worship in proper European fashion but couldn’t because someone had nicked the precious Angelus bell that called them to prayer.

“Where is the bell?” Joey the Indian wanted to know.

With the exception of the quotation marks, that’s exactly what I wrote. I know this because my mother produced the yellowed pages for all to mock.

Had I paid attention I might have known that Joey was not a typical 18th-century name for an Indian boy. Neither was Margie, which is what I named the Indian girl who answered him with, “Some very bad masked man must have stole it.”

“Ronald the bad man,” I continued all those long years ago, “had stole the bell and was going to melt it down for gold.”

Ronald, no less! And who makes bells out of gold? Never mind, I plunged ahead, eventually leading my perfectly holy little L.A. Indians to the foot of a cross where they naturally prayed certain-to-be-well-received little prayers for the return of their beloved bell.

“God heard them and told Ronald the bad to give the bell back again or he would be in trouble and he did and the children got the bell back and were so happy they sang and prayed and the mission was named Lost Angelus so everyone would remember forever this holy miracle sent from heaven ... The end.”

Under my beautifully executed story Sister Mary wrote in letters that nearly sliced the lined paper, “Mrs. Bogert, John will stay after school for five days to atone for his willfully poor work!"

"It was the best story in class and willfully so!" I said, when the laughter subsided.

"You haven't changed one single bit," said my wife.

And me, I am happy to live far away from all this, in a secret place that I shall forever call Lost Angelus.

He's going to the dogs, and enjoying every moment of it

August 12, 1988

I'm not a dog person.

Guys who own dogs, real dogs, have names like Helmut.

Helmut is a man who can say, "Sit!" with authority. He knows where to buy a good studded dog collar.

While I don't generally spend my days in a kimono and fluffy slippers, I never felt up to the task of owning any animal that's bigger than a car.

Then there is Clifford.

Actually, there was just this big dog at the pound, a sheep dog kind of creature, beige as a rental store couch and a jerk if there ever was one.

I was within the fragrant confines of the pound only because my daughter's art class ran late and happened to be across the street. I could hear it and smell it, so why not have a look?

Inside, the usual collection of dog riffraff barked, cavorted and otherwise behaved like, well, like dogs. But among the half-breeds, part-breeds, no-breeds and horror-show-canine-quadroons was this beige thing with a giant shag.

He looked like his socks needed pulling up, a field

to run in, a Walt Disney camera to perform for, a kid to chase, a cat to torment and a good shampoo.

"Nice dog," I said to a pound employee who was not so happily hosing out a cage. "It says on the tag here that he's an Old English sheep dog mix?"

"He's mixed all right," the hoser quipped.

As I said, I'm not a dog guy. But I am stupid, so I put my hand in the cage. Five minutes later, it was still inside the wire, still attached to my wrist and embedded in the fur of a dog that wouldn't let go. He licked me. Like a grizzly, he stood and rubbed against the fence uprights. He did everything but ask for a crooked lawyer and enough cash to spring him.

"What do I know from dogs?" I reasoned, pulling myself back from the brink. "OK, then, give him a manly command."

"Sit," I said, a panzer captain's steel in my voice. He didn't. "Lie down," I implored. He wouldn't.

Forget it. I left, but over the days the dog dribbled into my thoughts and conversation. "Maybe I'll go have another look," I told my wife.

"Uh-huh," she replied, exhibiting her usual concern for my many interests.

On the following Saturday I again visited the beast that had already been named (sight unseen) Clifford by my 5-year-old, who has been trying to hang that name on a pet—even a female kitten—since she read it in a storybook.

"Well, did you get Clifford?" was the question I heard for the rest of that day after spending another half-hour petting the beast.

"No," I replied, because, well, because I'm not a dog guy. And I remained so until the following Saturday, when I again visited Clifford and asked the keeper if we might free him for a moment.

"It's your life. He's been in stir for nearly two months,"

the man said, going off to find a (no kidding) adoption counselor.

"I'll put a leash on him, but he'll act weird," the counselor said. Then she added cryptically, "He's running out of time."

Clifford pulled me around like a cartoon character. Still, I liked him, but I wasn't taking him home without a family decision.

"Him?" my wife asked when we returned en masse to the pound later that day. "This is Clifford? We'll take him. You there ... " She stopped a passing adoption counselor with an authoritative tone. "We'll take this animal."

My little girl, Rachael, patted his head (keeping in mind that he is a full head taller than her sitting down) and called him, "A big, good dog."

So Clifford—an already neutered stray with no known past—became ours. But not before we signed a paper promising that we would keep this foolish, jumping, crazed animal until he either calmed down or we all died.

First order of business was a bath. Second order of business was getting to know him, an easy task considering Clifford's basic nature; Clifford, it seems, loves the world and everything in it.

We soon found that Clifford, only a year or two old himself, lets small children sleep on him. Clifford will wear a Dodgers cap for a kids' game and will sleep bedside and "woof!" when he hears strange sounds. Clifford will stay close when you are trying to write bad fiction. And Clifford does not care if you use him for a foot rest. Clifford loves to jog and chase old tennis balls that he forgets to return. Clifford is so sweet and dumb that he makes absolutely everyone feel like a genius.

Best of all, Clifford is always happy to see me, even if I've been gone only a minute, even if my name isn't Helmut and even if I bought him a nice red collar instead of one bearing metal studs.

Although I have come to all this at a late age, it would seem that there is something inside Clifford that completes an ancient bond. No cat mystery here, no feline aloofness, just (dare I say it?) a very good friend.

Daughter's birthday party truly is a celebration of life

August 29, 1988

My luck, our luck, or maybe it's Rachael's own luck that has held for two years.

"We've gotten her this far," I'll allow.

Watch those fates and remember that the realm of potential loss is nowhere to dwell except for those days when one is forced, by the presence of cakes and party hats bearing the image of Donald Duck, to stop and consider.

As my younger child Rachael celebrated her second birthday Thursday evening, I found myself (or maybe I put myself there on purpose, who knows) grilling hot-dogs on the exact spot where we once did some suffering together.

The heat is what I remember. Since then I have associated heat radiating off this piece of concrete at the far end of our pool with the first disquieting moment that I exposed her tiny body—having just arrived in the world a full month early—to the sun.

I covered her eyes with gauze strips and knew that my late Italian grandmother, figuring age from conception onward, would have said the child was 8 months old.

By my way of thinking she was less than new. She

was early to the party, and nobody was ready for her. My wife was in bed and the baby's new body parts, like a suddenly released prisoner's, hadn't yet adjusted to life on the outside.

She was jaundiced. And though that is not unusual in newborns, to a premature baby weighing well under 5 pounds, that (and almost everything else about her) seemed life-threatening.

Her spine, resting against the flat of my hand was like thread, like what you'd expect to feel pushing out from a kitten. Nothing about her was fully formed, even her voice was tentative.

Out there in the sun, where I had taken her so the ultraviolet light could combat the jaundice, I'd notice things about her. She had no eyebrows or eyelashes and her eyes, when open, looked—like mine, I am sure—absolutely lost.

My 4-year-old daughter would sometimes sit with us and touch the baby's hands and ask the question I'd ask myself over and over: "Is she going to live?"

"Of course," I'd say. But I had no way of knowing.

It didn't help that I was exhausted and that absolutely everyone would remark that this was the smallest baby they'd ever seen.

What I didn't know—though I suspect that my wife was well aware of it—was the fact that Rachael had her own ideas about life. The cry she let out when I returned her to the hospital for a blood test—they punctured the bottom of her inch-long foot—should have given me vision. I should have been able to see her at age 2 opening a box containing a Cobra gun-ship and screaming at the older children, "This is my helicopter. Get away!"

But dads, unlike small babies and the uncanny women that bear them, can be of a doubting sort. These days I wonder if Rachael wasn't willed into existence by her mother and—where is the medical evidence on this?—herself.

I had a terrible case of hospital-bred flu and the newborn baby had a heart valve problem that corrected itself, as predicted by her doctor, on what should have been her due date. Still, I had plenty of time to sit at the pool's edge talking to her, my hand covering her entire chest, with our big black cat looking on.

It is difficult to admit it even now, but the fear of losing her kept me, emotionally and for a very short time, at a slight distance. I did all the things that I was supposed to do but the fragility of this tiny life, the feeling that it could vanish like breath in cold air, petrified me.

Though all distance between us—save my own guilt—has long since vanished, I still suspect Rachael Rose willed herself here and that will is iron. Talky as a parrot, she is all command and absolutely fearless physical interjection.

At one point during her party she threw open her arms and announced: "My friends!"

It was so strange to stand where I had experienced despair and see triumph as she ripped blocks, a jacket, an airplane, a puzzle, shirts and dresses from their wrappings saying "Thanks! Where's more?"

When everyone had gone I sat close to her, close enough to smell the cake and ice cream on her clothes and hear her little sing-song humming as she played with a new toy.

"How was it, kid?" I asked, my hand on her back.

"Rachael's birthday!" she proclaimed, emphatically thumping herself on the chest. "Rachael's birthday!"

So it is, my wonderful girl, so it is.

Feeling more like the dummy in an interview with Edgar Bergen

September 21, 1989

You have to admire a grown woman remembering her departed dad. There was Candice Bergen, picking up an Emmy in Pasadena and closing with, "Dad, if you're watching, this is for you."

Really, that was a touching moment, speaking as it did to the Shinto-like love many of us have for departed parents. Of course, her dad was Edgar Bergen, ventriloquist and founding president of the Academy of Television Arts and Sciences, the group that hands out the very Emmy that Candice took home.

What caught me was the joy in her voice, the kind of joy a dad can give a daughter, a dad that I once spent a curious afternoon with many years ago in my first California interview. I had only recently hired onto a daily newspaper and was, after months of starvation, still feeling honored to have work.

I was even more pleased to be assigned the Bergen interview because I had grown up in the 1950s with great respect for ventriloquists. And there were a number of them around back then. They made good television, which was new and primitive.

Bergen, of course, had been around long before television, in movies and on the radio. But why anyone would listen to a ventriloquist on the radio is beyond me. How could you tell if he was moving his lips?

Anyway, Bergen threw his voice well.

I just wish he had started throwing earlier that day in his Bel-Air home, which was huge and austere as a dentist's office, with glass walls and polished stone floors.

And Bergen wasn't much warmer. After answering the door himself we sat face to face, the entertainer answering all my questions with a curt "yes" or "no." No elaboration, no humorous anecdotes, no humor. We're talking the reporter's nightmare, the dreaded Stepford Interview.

After 15 minutes with this zombie, my shirt was sweat-soaked. What am I saying? My tie was sweat-soaked. How, I began to wonder in my panic, was I going to tell my new boss that I couldn't get the story?

"It's you," I accused myself. "Here's a man who knew Chaplin, a man who knew W.C. Fields and you can't get him to cut loose with even one funny story. Idiot, jerk. God, there's no air in the room. I'm dying!"

"What was W.C. Fields like?" I heard myself asking.

He thought for a long minute. "Nice," he said.

"Nice. W.C Fields—nice," I wrote, in my notebook.

That was it. I was finished, washed up.

"Well," I lied, looking for an escape route. "I guess I have what I need."

"Would you like to meet Charlie?" he suddenly deadpanned.

"Charlie McCarthy. Yes. I guess I would." Please God,

get me out of here alive!

In a moment he was back from a walk-in safe with his wooden buddy on his arm. Then events took one of those weird tilts. That piece of hollowed-out tree started ridiculing me, telling Bergen I looked like an Arab who somehow missed the oil boom and that I was far too thin and shy and obviously not too bright.

"What, are you a dummy?" the dummy asked me, and I almost didn't hear because I was laughing while Bergen corrected and apologized for his friend's behavior.

"Really, I am terribly sorry about Charlie's manners. He has learned nothing over the years, nothing at all," Bergen said, as Charlie attacked relentlessly: a wooden Don Rickles who was easily the most animated object in the room.

I stayed for two hours talking to Charlie about life in a trunk and early Hollywood. And when I left, I shook Charlie's hand, only stopping myself in the driveway.

"Nice meeting you, too, Mr. Bergen," I called as Charlie continued to heckle, railing on the other side of the closed door as I started my car and returned to the office to profile a dummy.

Years later I'd read an interview with Candice Bergen where she mentioned how dad would bring Charlie in to wish her goodnight. Obviously, Candice didn't forget her father. And neither will I. Not in this life I won't.

Anyone want to buy a $20 sort-of sheep dog, even cheaper?

November 21, 1989

I probably would have been thinking more cogently about the task at hand—recovering a slobbering, 90-pound, beige sheep dog—had Saturday night's entertainment not bled into Sunday morning.

But I had been asleep, having entered that state full of trepidation. For I knew, as do all parents who linger too long at the ball, that the children will rise like Godzilla at 7 sharp no matter what the condition of your head.

For two full hours I had slept the sleep of the dead, until a cold, wet, awful, disgusting thing touched my face.

Only partially roused from the nether world, I wondered, has death finally come?

No. This wet death also had a tongue and breath as foul as hell's own hound. I am licked on eyes, mouth, ears. Don't take me now, Lord, I just ain't ready.

"Ruff!" Oh great, God is a dog, an anagram after all.

"Ruff!" Wait, that sounds so familiar. Open the eyes, yes, there in the light: Behold the pale beast Clifford with his great, feather-like tale wagging. His head drops, then up it comes to deposit a frog-shaped squeaky toy—his only earthly possession—right under my horizontal nose.

"Lemme guess," I said, "you want to go out?"

Out, of course, was the key word and as important in Clifford's limited universe as the words walk and dinner.

He was excited as we walked together out the front door. And there I stood watching the massive beast sniffing around the ice plant for I don't know what: A dog that passed this way in 1948, his lost family, the missing link that would once and for all prove a genetic connection between man and hound?

What did I expect from a $20 pound dog?

Did I mention that I was wearing pajamas, something I started doing because I have small daughters and because, well, because I'm supposed to. Still, nice as these particular pajamas are with their sweet pattern of stars and moons on a light blue background, I still feel like a 7-year-old in them.

Just then a coyote ran past. Or maybe it wasn't a coyote. Maybe it was just a fast gray dog.

Did I mention that Clifford's only fault—apart from a lack of brain power—is his hatred of all dogs except himself and May-May, the rat pup from next door?

Well, he knows May-May. And the gray ghost flying past at 3:30 Sunday morning was not her.

In a nonce, or half a nonce, Clifford was gone. He may be a big jerk, but he is a fast one. The sight of such a large, feathery beast running full-throttle across the lawn and down our long street was enough to make a man gasp in wonder, "That's one fast doggie."

Then, naturally, that same man would have to think: "My dog just ran away and I'm standing here like a dork in little-kid pajamas."

That's when I began one of those pursuits that can only make a biped feel completely inadequate. The faster I ran barefoot across lawns and deserted sidewalks wet with ground fog, the farther away Clifford—a bounding, ghostly white blob under the distant street lamps—seemed to be.

I would have called out, but that would have brought out the neighbors and I didn't want them to see me dressed in clothing substitutes. So I ran hard and had actually covered two blocks when the police car pulled alongside me. It's odd, but when kids are running double-A fuel dragsters down my street, these guys are nowhere to be found.

Here it was, 3:30 on a moonlit morning and there he was. Excuse me, there she was. In fact, there were two of them, both women in uniform in the squad car's front seat.

"Lost?" the cop riding shotgun asked. There was a touch of humor in her voice, like the heavily armed pair of them were about to break into the sort of female laughter that drives men to seek exile in bowling alleys and bottles.

"My dog ran after a coyote . . . or something," I replied, trying to look casual in my silly pajamas in front of two uniformed, and obviously too young to be out at this hour, women. They didn't reply. "I'm serious, he's down the street somewhere, probably being eaten if we're really lucky."

"Name?" the officer monotoned.

"Clifford."

"Last name?"

"Sorry, Clifford's my dog's name."

"Color?"

"A sort of naturally filthy beige."

"Does he have long fur?" she suddenly asked. "And a huge tail?"

"Yes, yes, that's what he looks like exactly!" I replied, thinking they already had an APB or a DOA, or whatever they call it, out on him.

"There he is," she said, as the hideously happy beast came trotting up, first to me then over to the policewoman, where he offered his hairy head and behaved in the most obsequious way.

"You idiot!" I said. The policewoman sat suddenly upright, her gun hand still on Cliffie's wet snout. "Sorry, not you, the dog."

She smiled a beguiling smile. "Good night, sir," she said. "Nice dog."

"Yes, I plan to sell him to for scientific experimentation."

"And sir?"

"Yes."

"Nice jammies."

Hillside vista recalls how society failed dead young girl

January 9, 1990

Among many other things, it was a bit of upholstery fiber in the eye of a dead girl that nailed Angelo Buono. Along with his adopted cousin, a legendary creep named Kenneth Bianchi, the auto upholsterer cut a horrifying swath through L.A. County during 1977 and 1978.

Together, they were known as the Hillside Strangler. Of course, back in the early morning hours of October 31, 1977, nobody could conceive of two guys with the same bent: Picking up young girls, then raping, torturing and strangling them before dumping their bodies on hillsides in the Glendale area.

That's where I met Judith Lynn Miller. The young, blond, runaway-turned-prostitute had been dead a few hours from what the coroner would call ligature strangulation.

"What's that?" I asked weeks later, sounding like a complete fool.

"Ligature, a cord," the coroner's spokesman replied. "You new on the job?"

In fact, I was. And the happenings on that particularly fine morning in the unincorporated hillside community of La Crescenta proved to me how new and unready, as most of us are for the truly horrific, I was.

Not surprisingly, I had put the event away entirely until Sunday morning. Another fine beginning in paradise, and I was driving past that same street on the way to visit a friend.

There it was, the Spanish-style house, the same small stucco archway out front and the ivy. Nothing had changed. And, I guess, nothing will ever change as long as there are people to remember the young girl, lying blue-skinned and naked in the ivy, partially covered by a blue tarpaulin, then uncovered completely, 20 yards distant, but close enough to see her stricken gaze.

I was working for a small paper in Glendale back then. It was my first California newspaper job and it was my duty to cover, among other things, the Crescenta Valley sheriff's station.

Coming from a Florida paper where down-scale, impossible-to-sympathize-with drug killings were common, this seemed like life in the dead letter office: Nothing here but amateur breaking and entering ("perpetrator allegedly absconded with one 10-speed bicycle and a collection of Playboy magazines") and me on the verge of collapse from boredom.

Maybe I even wished something big would happen just before it did, first thing in the morning, with a call from an equally bored deputy on the morning shift.

"We got a dead girl," the desk cop said, giving me the address. "Don't tell anybody I told you."

That was the beginning of a two-year roller coaster ride during which Buono killed at least nine young girls and his cousin another five, plus two in Washington state.

Looking back across the yellowing news clip, it's amazing to see how large loomed the shadows of these two unremarkable losers. In Torrance, in Westchester, practically everywhere in the county, young women "ke-yaad!" in karate classes. They banged away at pistol ranges and were filled with quotable paranoia: "I'm small, blond and 18," said a Redondo Beach woman in an April 1979 story. "I could be next."

Still, what were her chances of being grabbed in an area containing maybe 2 million young, blond women? Chances of freeway death were far greater, but such is the magic of fear and the certain knowledge that a man, a Hillside Strangler (teeth dripping blood, vile hands crossing and uncrossing a ligature) had marked you as his prey.

Meanwhile, the police put 100 men on what would be called, at first, the Los Angeles Strangler. Years later, Norm Jacoby, the venerable old war horse of City News Service and the man who eventually named the Hillside Strangler, the Night Stalker and many other geeks of note, said it took him longer than usual to name this one.

"It needed," he said with a curious laugh, "the proper ring."

After hundreds of false starts and not a few false arrests, the police got their men. Bianchi, true to his character, gave evidence enough against his cousin and avoided the gas chamber. Both men got life without parole.

They're in jail now, receiving visitors, eating, watching television, reading and breathing. I know somebody who saw Buono recently in the big vending machine-stocked visitors room at a famous Northern California prison.

He seemed, I was told, a happy enough man as he ate Doritos.

Sunday morning, it again seemed unfair. Worst of all is this feeling that I carry around, the one that tells me that I never conveyed—not completely or in any meaningful way—what it was like to see that girl so naked and defenseless, only 16 but failed utterly by everyone.

When the police finished with Judith Miller, the coroner's men loaded her body onto a wheeled stretcher.

Her hair—a shade of blond that might have once looked pretty against a party dress or a new wool sweater—fell across the white sheet and caught the sun.

Then she was gone.

A tribute to Pa Boling, and all the Pa Bolings we knew

July 24, 1990

A few years ago, my mother-in-law—who was then in her late 50s—became an orphan.

She hadn't expected feelings of abandonment when her aged mother died. But there they were: The girl inside the woman was now parentless. She was suddenly alone in the world. And never mind that she had her own pretty children and grandchildren; she had lost the last living link to her own beginning.

Then came an even more depressing thought. She was next in line.

Except for a small cousin who died suddenly in the 1930s of meningitis, everyone in her once-large family had gone down in the proper order: Great-grandparents, grandparents, mothers, fathers, daughters, sons.

If "The End" had to be typed across the bottom of the page, this was the best way to do it—by age and generation.

Still, knowing you're the next over the top can drive even strong people to religion, or worse.

Of course, this is all subjective. I mean, who exactly are our parents? Who, for instance, was my father? The guy who walked out when I was 7, the stepfather who raised me and gave me his name or—and this is a swim into murky waters—the other grown men who filled in the gaps by just being there and being terribly square.

I have lost both of my real fathers. And time isn't being terribly kind to those who lived.

Ancient coaches and great old Italians with stogie breaths have vanished. Tremendous life forces forever gone except for passing images in the dead of night when reality and weird memory do their awful thing.

A younger man, not being admired by an older man, is a younger man being hurt, a half-bright philosopher once said.

I don't know if that's absolutely true. But it seemed true to me when I tried to add up the people left in this world who could still look upon me as a young man or youngish man or a man with any possibilities at all.

I started down that slippery path when William Boling (Pa Boling, I called him) suffered a heart attack a couple of weeks ago. He's OK, or as OK as a man in his 70s can be who has just had a heart attack.

His son, my closest friend since we were both 14, called with the news. There I was, looking down the great abyss once again, recalling all the kindnesses lavished on me as a boy by this most southern of gentlemen.

It's a curse of perception, this inability to see the great care that went into our development until someone mentions that one of the care-givers is ill.

My friend and I spoke in pop medical terms, sharing half-knowledge and ignorance about heart attacks, EKGs and tissue damage while I recalled the early years.

Pa Boling was a World War II bomber pilot, yacht broker, businessman and real estate agent. Best of all, he was a grand cook in the grand tradition of his Louisiana boyhood.

There was fried chicken to die for and tamales assembled from the finest components: corn husks from Arizona, meal from Texas and napalm from Dow chemical.

My inability to swallow those torchlike tamales became a family legend. Just as legendary, in my mind, was Pa Boling making a separate, more mild batch for me—a too-thin kid from up the block who had fallen in for a lifetime with his son.

Through junior high and all through high school, college and beyond, Pa Boling's magic kitchen was my second home. There were times when it felt like my first home.

Then there was the influence of this genuine old boy, a man who never swore around women and would never tell an unclean joke in the presence of his wife.

We never know where our influence begins or ends. And only in extreme moments are we aware of our fragility and of the fact that all of life's grand structures are sadly temporary.

I'm sure Pa Boling never meant to influence me in any way at all. But he did. And how can I repay what I internalized so early on, except to say thanks, many thanks, and pass it on.

If he did the right thing, how come he feels so wrong?

March 27, 1992

I'll lay this out and let you decide because I'm as baffled by this rotten century's dead-end—especially the right and wrong of it—as you are.

And what, in all this, is more baffling than the way we treat children. Or the way certain creeps treat children. Not that the behavior of others was more than 99 percent at fault for what I felt Wednesday evening as Clifford (my sheeplike dog) and I took our evening run.

We were groaning along the street we live beside in darkness. About a mile up that street is an elementary school. In front of that school was a child, probably a sixth-grader.

Later, the police dispatcher would ask, "How old is a sixth-grader?"

That, obviously, was someone who doesn't have children, someone well apart from that time in the parental half-life when all kids come in grades rather than ages. Me, I have a K and a 4. But that's getting ahead of the story.

When I passed the child, I smiled. But I did not smile overly long because children, as is right, are told from birth to avoid strangers. And I make a conscious effort not to be the nice stranger that takes down a kid's highly justified guard.

She was sobbing, this possible sixth-grader, standing alone in the dark in front of a locked-tight school rubbing her eyes with her jacket cuff.

"What do we do now, Cliff?" I asked the dog as we moved along.

On the ancient right/wrong level—the one I grew up in, the one that still lives inside us, the one we bypass like a bad artery because the world has gone so tragically weird—I should have stopped instantly.

Look, I hate to make too much of the Italian thing I grew up with mainly because that Italian thing also gave us John Gotti.

But rough as the old neighborhood was, a kid wouldn't have been left outside like that. Children were held apart from all that particular craziness. And they still should be, damn it. How could I let a little kid suffer?

We turned back and stopped, keeping a distance.

"Are you waiting for someone?" I asked, gentle-voiced, knocking down her guard and feeling strange about it.

"They haven't come," she said, more tears, more mopping at eyes that were nearly invisible in the darkness.

She had been there, she said, since the 2:40 p.m. bell. It was now 6:30. "Could I call someone for you?" Yes. "Can you write out a phone number?" She'd write two of them after fumbling in her pack for a pen and a small address book with pink flowers printed on the cover—real little-girl stuff. Boy, do I know about little-girl stuff.

"I'll run home and call for you. Stay calm," I said, knowing that the old neighborhood rules are dead. With my wife away until Saturday, there was no inviting her home. Heck, even if she was there, I couldn't and shouldn't move a strange child anywhere unless the sky itself was falling.

Now listen to the paranoia that descended upon me

as I ran home. What if something happened to her? I pictured a neighbor telling the police that they did see a girl but, wisely, decided to do nothing. But there was a tall man with a beige sheep dog. . .

At home I called the numbers. One was her best friend and she couldn't help because her parents weren't home. The other brought an old woman, or a drunk woman, or an old and drunk woman who told me that "the people" who were supposed to pick the child up couldn't find the school and she didn't know if they would be able to.

Great. I called the police. "Is this a Hispanic child?" the dispatcher asked. No, black. "African American," corrected the dispatcher. "How old?" A sixth-grader.

Twenty minutes later a cop young enough to be my son but old enough to wear what I'd call a "You're not a cop so you must be a creep" look, turned up at the door.

First thing out of his mouth, "Does that dog bite?" He was looking at a beast who looks like a Muppet. No. Suddenly he seemed to fixate on the left pocket of my shirt which happened to be embroidered with a large golf club and an outline of a beer bottle. "You called about a little girl?" Yes. "She's not at the school. Do you have any idea if she was picked up?" No. I just didn't want her left out there. You see, I have young daughters. And what is it about cops that they always make me feel so guilty?

"Is there a little girl in there?" the cops asked the older of the two girls who had joined me in the open doorway.

"Just her and she belongs here," she replied, pointing to her little sister.

"Mind if we come in and look around?" he asks, hand still on that gun.

I'm not a lawyer but I do know that once you allow police into your house they can do pretty much anything they like. "No, you can't come in. Look, officer, should I have called you in the first place? Should I have just let that kid stand there in the dark? Should I have walked her down here?"

"We'll check it out," he replied after a pause, after looking me up and down again. I'm in sweat pants, sandals and the ridiculous, middle-age-guy golf shirt my in-laws gave me. I am, in short, the very picture of the brainless citizen/suspect.

They leave.

"Dad?" my 9-year-old asks. "Are we going to jail?"

Of course not.

But I did do the right thing, didn't I?

Male addition to the family won't be a Tom, Dick or Harry

August 3, 1993

I liked the name Charlotte. And I very nearly liked the idea of another girl in my life. It was the thought of an actual baby that troubled me.

Babies, they say (when they are at a safe distance), bring their love with them. And I guess they do. But why can't they be more like colts or whale calves, able to run and swim immediately. Why do human babies, among all creatures, remain so ridiculously helpless for so long?

Don't get me wrong, I like children. I just wish they'd arrive a year old and able to walk, eat solid food and sleep for more than two hours at a time.

I also wished—expected even—that this baby would arrive being Charlotte, the third of my little girls. Face it, we're set up for girls, with the girl clothes, the million-dollar Barbie collection, the hardly worn pink tennis shoes and the red cowboy boots my oldest daughter conned her mother into buying when she was three.

I have a photo of her wearing those boots in the pool.

Then there is fear to consider, a fear that is never much greater than when your wife is having a needle inserted into her abdomen, from which amniotic fluid is drawn for study and—as a fun side attraction—for determining sex.

But I didn't have to wait for test results. No, we had a smart doctor, a handsome woman who took the fluid, then cast about with an electronic wand imaging the baby on a television screen.

There it was, baby on radar—a rotating head-scratching thumb-sucking ghost compilation of bones and organ flux that could, if you looked at it just right, resemble a disorderly flock of 747s stacked over LAX.

"Want to know your baby's sex?" the doctor asked, casual as hell.

"It's a girl. We specialize in girls," I said.

Actually, we didn't mean to specialize in yet another girl—even one to fill the Charlotte vacancy—at this time in our lives. My wife is still at a reasonable time of life, but I'm heading into at-your-age? land, the place where Mick Jagger and other half-mad geezers dwell.

After all, I have done this before. WE have done this before and the magic, as it must, has begun to pall. More midnight feeds, more unexplained temperatures, diapers (cloth or disposable?), feeding (breast or bottle?), school (start early or hold back?), yet another girl to teach a language and belabor with numerals. Another girl. . . .

"It's a boy," the doctor announced.

"What?"

"That isn't the umbilical," she condescended, pointing to a small but familiar shape on radar. "And that isn't his finger."

Wait. If it's not a finger it must be ...

"We don't have a boy's name," I said moronically, poleaxed—bye-bye Charlotte.

"Brendan is good," the doctor suggested, like we had suddenly turned Irish. "Brian is also popular."

My wife came up with Ian Henry. Ian, in the fading language of her ancient homeland, means John—my name, her father's name, my grandfather's name and the name of her first boyfriend, The Doctor—though she swears that this has nothing to do with anything.

Henry comes from our dear friend Henry Watson, a nobleman if there ever was one. And I can hear the combination, "Where's Ian Henry?"

Heck, a kid with a name like that could be anywhere; up a tree, shooting skeet, learning to cook, writing a book or playing with his sisters.

Ian Henry is a boy and—if the male gods of old are willing—bound to enter this sad world at about the point in my life-arc where the throwing arm plays out and when a failure to get eight hours' sleep makes me spend the next 16 doing a Boris Karloff impression.

A boy, can you imagine, ordained by science and my last Y-chromosome; a boy spoken of as existing somewhere off yonder, a boy due to arrive from somewhere else. But if he isn't here now, then my wife is hosting an unsanctioned kick-boxing match in the center of her body.

Come November, they say, and I will be the father of a son who will never know me as young.

I have a thousand dismal thoughts just like that one. Only at odd moments—like the recent day when I caught a matchlessly beautiful vision of the sea down slanting streets—it occurred to me that I would soon be showing all this to my boy, my son, to my little Ian, whoever he may be.

Cribbing a cot for our new arrival

September 28, 1993

A baby in its liquid universe is not reality. OK, maybe it is for some people, especially if those people happen to be pregnant women. But to a guy, some solid preparation is required to translate the feel of that internal soccer match into approaching reality.

Too bad "approaching" to an expectant mother and a far less expectant father mean such different things.

Her view: We have only five weeks left!

His view: In dogs years, five weeks is practically forever.

She, meanwhile, has purchased diapers and has laundered all the male-approximate articles of clothing that could be culled from plastic sacks of ridiculously tiny garments worn by both our daughters and the children of at least three friends.

"When are you going to assemble the cot?" the expecting one asked.

Luckily, I happen to know that "cot" is the British word for crib. Otherwise, I might be heading down to the surplus store looking for God only knows what. "When?" I asked. "Gosh, with five weeks to go, maybe the end of October."

Actually, it was going to be right then, which was Saturday morning when I had it in mind to do a little writing on my elegant new personal computer.

Here's how the conversation went: Tomorrow. NOW! Later. NOW! In an hour? NOW! Maybe now.

Next to the grizzly bear, the pregnant human is the most threatening creature in all of nature. Really, entire animal kingdom shows have been dedicated to just this subject.

Plus, I had a reason for all this foot-dragging, and it had to do with the 11-year- old crib's location in our tiny, dusty cellar and (can you spot the key word in this sentence?) with the fact that I knew it had to be completely reassembled.

I know because I disassembled it after the last kid. Not only that, I clearly recalled tossing out the instruction book, because I just knew that we'd never need it again, ever.

Yeah, well, the only thing clear about my life is the fact that there is nothing terribly clear about it.

By noon I was hauling the crib pieces up. But this is no ordinary crib. It's one of those twin-bed contraptions that converts into a crib. And it was all right there, the chest of drawers that sits at one end and the crib sides that hold it to the changing table that rests at the other end.

Still, I had to ask: Why did I save the major components and toss out the screws and the instructions. Did I half want a third baby? Or am I just an idiot?

Luckily, since I first assembled this monster, industry has given us the cordless drill and the PC, not that a PC could do anything but sit quietly in the nursery-to-be reminding me that this wonderful sun-filled space has ceased to be my own.

Along with the cordless drill and my advancing years came the invention of the drywall screw and a certain amount of impatience that was not there when I first lovingly fitted this crib together. Ah, the memory of complete ignorance. The thought of a sweet little head resting in a space created with my own hands . . . For get about it. Let me tell you, with drywall screws and a cordless drill a guy could piece together an ocean liner. The things will go through stone, I swear. And they went through the wood of this crib like butter.

Is this where the top piece goes? Who cares, GRRRRRRR-SQUEAL.

Take that!

I could see by the old holes that four screws originally held each side in place. HA! Four! I laugh at four. I spit at four. Stick eight of them in. The more the merrier. Oh, you don't want to stay upright. A wise guy. Try 20 of my razor-tipped black, titanium (don't you just love that word?) fasteners.

Under this massive metal onslaught the crib gave in. Maybe some of you don't believe that certain objects have minds of their own or that they don't contrive ways to thwart assembly.

Well, if you think that, then you've never pieced together something on this scale, something that actually has to be assembled so a baby doesn't come to harm.

It's a funny thing. But the more screws I put into it and the sturdier it became—arriving eventually at nearly bulletproof baby cage—the more I started picturing the little guy in it; my son, stinking, crying and generally filling the place with hope.

Son's birth nothing less than epiphany for joyous parents

November 7, 1993

"Baby?"

"Certainly."

"Noonish?"

"Lovely."

"See you then."

"Ciao."

As a veteran of two all-night baby-birthing sessions, I can attest to the utterly civilized planned C-section performed at noon. Gives a guy plenty of time for breakfast and the paper before birth.

Cut, hack, ba-boom! We had Ian Henry.

There's the kid, darn near eight pounds of future column subject covered in unspeakable gore, his slate-colored eyes trying to focus on his mom dressed out like a Christmas goose and a bunch of masked men looking for all the world like the Dalton Gang.

Only seconds before, we men had been discussing the relative merits of Klingons, Vulcans and such. We were even telling jokes. But my wife, bless her supine, sheet-covered self, was not joining in the fun.

Rather rude, I thought, because she was conscious through all the hacking and carving and asking the most irrelevant questions. I can't remember them all, but "Did somebody just cut me open?" and "Is the baby OK?" comes to mind.

"Sure, it's all fine. You just lay back and relax," I said, when they paused with the hacking and cutting and allowed me to take a few snapshots and cut the umbilical cord. This is some bit of work too, the umbilical. Goodyear should figure out how to make tires this both-hands-on-the-scissors tough.

Anyway, I'm standing there some few feet removed from my wife, trying to describe a creature that is changing in color and form by the second like something from special effects. He came out kind of blue but went pink quickly as his little smushed-down face popped out like a can of Bud.

In no time at all he looked exactly like . . .

"Who does he look like?" asked my wife, who at that moment was getting into the spirit of things after doing a knock-down impression of that guy in "Alien," the one that explodes all over the dinner table.

"Well?" I stalled, knowing precisely who the baby looked like but fearing to speak the name.

"Well?" she demanded.

"Remember 'The Godfather?'"

"Yes."

"He looks like Fat Clemenza."

It later was determined that he looked more like George III of England. It also was determined later that babies, as my mother-in-law assured me, bring their love with them. This is the same mother-in-law who, noting her five granddaughters and hearing of little Ian Henry's birth by long-distance, said: "The line of queens is broken."

That sounds rather dramatic but birth is drama itself, even when accomplished at a civilized time of day. It was odd. No, it was damned odd, extremely odd, Jurassically colossally odd, in fact, to look at a clock and realize that the entire birth of wee Ian Henry took less than one Earth hour.

From parents of two to parents of three, from extreme promise-anything worry to just normal frantic parental worry, from not knowing someone at all to loving someone instantly, smiling, talking, doing all the things that add up to a bond that we hope will carry us through good times and bad and all in 55 minutes.

Most of all there is this feeling that comes with a successful birth, a feeling that no matter what happens in life or how we will eventually part, at least we have this moment between us. Despite all the troubles present and troubles to come, we can hold a baby close and, for a short time, allow ourselves to think that the world is not so rotten after all.

And birth, if you'll excuse the profusion of the well-used, is a miracle: a message from the unknown that we are—none of us—as bad as we think or ever more blessed.

Beach town takes personally the killing of its protector

January 4, 1994

The why of such tragedy is almost never known. There is usually only how and a gun, a killer and a victim.

Mostly we don't notice victims because they exist at a remove. There are city lines between us, color lines, distance. Any distance is comforting.

It takes a solid hit to bring it in the front door: a police officer, 29, good-looking, wide boyish smile, his nephew along for the drive, a cake-walk evening two days after Christmas; a guy in a crummy two-door compact committing some kind of traffic violation near the Manhattan Village mall.

Then came the gun and the vulnerable sick feeling the enemy brings to the gate.

Like Manhattan Beach itself, its police are generally not thought to be in the direct line of fire.

So this particularly brutal shooting shocked people who did not know the murdered officer, Martin Ganz, and it shocked even more the people who did know him for his kindness and devotion.

In his 29 years, the man earned superlatives and the kind of spontaneous tribute normally reserved for rock stars and the best politicians. It is all so simple, all so complex, all those flowers, a 35-foot-long tribute of votive candles, poems, signs, love and outrage laid out along a wall near the spot where he died.

It was suddenly our city and our lost man tragically juxtaposed against all those potted poinsettias and the rebirth they represent.

It was the same outside American Martyrs Church in Manhattan Beach on Monday morning where ancient reserves of tribute emerged for Martin Ganz: come into this world on July 13, 1964, gone from it on December 27, 1993.

The governor arrived, then the black-clad family was escorted across the crowded street past subdued news crews by uniformed police, their shields eloquently crossed with a line of black.

Just down the road waited lines of police cars while their many drivers stood in silent ranks, a brotherhood that understands a job that can so quickly and savagely take any one of them from wife, husband, children, a city, all of us. Take them and give us nothing back but a lesson, if we are lucky, and splendid show of dignity along with the certain knowledge that it will happen again.

Twenty rows of armed, gloved uniformed officers with bulletproof vests visible beneath triple-creased shirt backs—prepared as always. Always, as with us all, unprepared.

A black hearse at the curb, a coffin, a guitar plays softly through outdoor speakers, a dog barks on the far side of the wide parking lot, making the silence palpable.

In the crowd are people in shorts, mothers bouncing babies on their hips, people dressed well and people who have just wandered in as they were.

It's a small enough town where a dead policeman will cause a flag at Blockbuster Video to fly at half-staff.

It's the size town where people appreciate the men and women who guard the wall and where quiet appreciation can turn quickly into emotion that can itself turn into sobs over senseless death and the enormity of the sickness without.

This, after all, is the cop who brought Woody Woodpecker to the schools. Trying to teach safety, trying to hammer home the point that NO can be far better than YES. This is a cop who also was an uncle to 13 and the blessed son of Jeannine Ganz, beloved of Pamela Ham and the devoted brother of Radine Pobuda, Clarissa Eichar, Rachael Walker, Janet Chase and Mary Pfaff.

Think of Christmas with all those children. Think of the happy Christmas just past and this sudden horrible veering off. But Ganz is himself, a speaker reminds us, now free of pain and hatred.

Later, while the long motorcade escorted the dead officer to his grave, a young couple stood by the spot where he died.

They bent to touch the flowers and read the cards and when they stood they kissed as people will to comfort one another.

Togetherness, dogs and all, is only way to survive shaking

January 18, 1994

It isn't just a king-size bed. It's a California king-size, and I now know why it's called that, and why California, of all states, would have an extra-large bed named after itself.

I discovered this at 4:30 a.m. Monday when the earth went off under us, or close enough to under us that none of us really desired to be any closer.

Suddenly, we were being attacked by our own house.

More accurately, it was like a Keystone Kops film with my wife and I colliding at the foot of the big bed and deciding who was going after which of our children with that freight train noise all around and stuff breaking—ROARRRRRR! CRASH!

The joint creaked like the HMS Bounty, and my wife and I were operating on ancient instincts, running for the children, only to meet them head-on, getting jammed in the doorway with compact bodies and two very large dogs coming from the opposite direction.

When we sorted out those with fur from those without, we were only one short—the baby.

There is one, and only one good thing about babies. Babies, especially those less than three months old, do not yet know that houses are not supposed to shake like an Amtrak ride at 4:30 in the morning. They don't know that houses are supposed to be solid as rock, sheathed in copper, thick as steel-supported brick and safe, safe, safe.

The older children, being native to this strange place, know this is not normal, except in the way that it has become normal in their lives. It's the frightening cost of doing business.

Ian, the baby, was not crying. Or if he was, I could not hear him for the noise. Then I heard him. Laughing a liquid baby laugh.

Couldn't be. Couldn't be.

It could. It could.

In fact, it was. He was laughing like a loon at the clown mobile hanging over his crib. The room shook, the crib shook, and the roof timbers made threatening noises while the happy-faced clowns danced and jerked like old-time acid heads over his little coconut skull.

Babies are infinitely portable as well. And we all met up in the hallway, where a discussion began about the relative merits of standing in a doorway as opposed to standing in an open hall.

Doorway. Hall. Doorway. Hall. Doorway. Hall. My family is like a small convention of rabbinical students where no question is left to sit alone if it possibly can be forced to stand up and jump through hoops, even during an earthquake.

Finally, after what seemed like a mere 57 hours of shaking, it stopped.

"See, I was right," posed my lovely 11-year-old, who (don't ask me how) never looks more lovely than during times of crisis.

"Not!" rejoined her 7-year-old sister, a kid who actually seems to enjoy earthquakes.

"Whimper, whimper, sniffle, argh, whine," went the two large dogs, the worst of which was our Rodesian Ridgeback. I wouldn't mind the heavily muscled so-called Hound From Heck being a chicken of the worst sort. But the defining trait of a Rodesian Ridgeback is supposed to be courage. They are, after all, lion hunters.

Only the lion hunter was now on our California king-size bed, as close to me as my own skin, her sleek red doggie head on my pillow, her doggie breath in my face, her doggie tongue licking my nose with killer gratitude.

Elsewhere on the stadium-size pallet were two female children, a large sheep-like pound dog, my wife, a still smiling baby boy and the aforementioned cowardly lion killer.

Really, you should have come over, there was plenty of room.

Did I mention the burglar alarm?

Blending with the thundery sound of moving earth came the ear-shattering wooga-wooga-wooga noise of our alarm lending that red-alert feel one gets watching submarine movies.

I remembered the turn-off code but noticed, much later, that the alarm company didn't call to see if we were OK.

Finally, we were all snuggled in like a family of Cro-Magnons when the power failed. The lights were off and the aftershocks were still coming, but we knew the power had failed because our high-tech alarm system makes this loud droning sound whenever it is removed from its energy source.

To turn the thing off one need only punch in a single-digit code. Simple stuff. A child could do it. In fact, a child did do it because I couldn't remember the code and was busily looking for the alarm instructions when my 7-year-old turned it off by hitting every number on the key pad (except the emergency one) until it stopped.

We finished the long hours until dawn in this way, in a great human/doggie heap, lucking out together and fending off the evil movement as we should, together.

Weekend with daughter plants seeds for lasting relationship

April 26, 1994

The weekend's activities began after ballet class Saturday morning when my 7-year-old, Rachael, changed into one of her god-awful outfits and said, "Let's go."

"You let her go out like that?" her mother would later ask.

Are there guys somewhere who actually notice right off what their daughters wear? At least I saw (finally) that she was dressed like something out of a Dickens novel as she rode the roller coaster at a local high school-fair until the sullen ride operator said, "Beat it, kid."

She was in a faded green flower-print dress that years ago had belonged to her older sister, red tennis shoes, purple socks with bunnies on the sides and—continuing the bunny theme—a fake rabbit fur purse that she wore across her chest el bandito style.

She looked wretched but cute, which is Rachael's world in a nutshell.

Unlike most of us, she is at ease in the world, a member of her own one-person royal family and likely to get away with the most outrageous behavior.

"What's wrong with him?" she laughed, exiting the roller coaster and dragging me toward the other rides in this floating, frazzled, greasy-bicycle-chain-driven mobile show.

It was the very essence of fly-by-night. Yet there I was moving at excessive speed with her on faded Slap-Happy Fun, Happy-Go-Pukey, the Bullet Train To Heck and the Ferris wheel. I was grateful for the hamster-driven Ferris wheel and happy when we won the goldfish.

That was in her weekend plan, too, winning goldfish at the fair for her aquarium. We won 10 of them by tossing pingpong balls into water-filled jars, and it cost only $52.

"Wasn't that great?" she asked in the car as she stuffed cotton candy into her horrible little mouth, held her fish in their plastic bag and asked,

"Garden tomorrow?"

The vegetable garden had been promised for three years. But it wasn't until this windy Sunday that we actually had cleared a patch of ground big enough for crops, or at least a cropette.

To plant a serious vegetable garden one needs a pick to break up hard ground, lots of mulch and a chatty little girl to accompany you to the nursery, where you can spend an hour selecting seeds marked "Easy to grow."

"Beets grow well," a bystander, one of those nice but annoying people who think children are adorable, in the seed section volunteered.

"Is she kidding?" the kid whispered to me. "Starving dogs won't eats beets."

The kid had a point. That's why we decided to go with what she liked best: corn, cucumbers, carrots and yellow squash with a package of lavender seeds for her mom. We also bought tomato plants but not until the woman from the seed rack asked, "Do you know how to plant those?"

"He does. He's Italian," the kid replied.

The fact is, being of the Italian persuasion, I do know how to plant tomatoes. It's a small skill learned from my grandfather 40 years ago and a small skill that I pass along to my little girl who, like many in our mutt line, shares this springtime need to put things into the ground.

In the end, the rows were not straight and the planting untidy. And in the end we had spent a good portion of two days together, two days that must have been good for her because she purposely missed a birthday party to do it, two days in which we discussed absolutely everything.

Dinosaurs, trees, favorite rides, luck—wasn't it nice that we could engage in sport gardening?—friends, jokes and planting lore.

I told her of my grandfather and of the arrow-straight rows he tilled in the rich earth and of how, believing that tomato plants were sensitive to the cigar residue on his fingers, he'd have me nip the bottom branches off the small plants before placing them in the holes.

I don't know if that's scientific fact or not. But I know this: The kid will pass it on.

Communing with family history and religious tradition

May 10, 1994

Saturday was about explanations and earrings—explaining to our non-Catholic friends what first Communion was all about while wondering how I could go on telling my elder daughter not to have her ears pierced when boys her age have.

And there was the first Communion lunch, an intimate little affair for six that somehow blossomed into a hoedown because the person being honored was Rachael, our nutty 7-year-old who is well-loved by adults, children and those who can appreciate a good side-show act.

It's not that Rachael is a sideshow act, but it's close. There's something—how shall we say this?—engaging (or irritating, take your pick) about a kid who spends her days walking the fine line between humor and incarceration.

As for first Communion, and unlike extreme unction, it's pretty much what it sounds like. Only the Catholics make a big deal out of it, which I suppose it is. But our many Jewish friends were confused until I described it as an extension of the Last Supper, which itself was a Passover Seder and, well, they got the idea.

Anyway, Rachael was dressed in white dress, white

shoes, white stockings and a little crown made of fresh-cut white roses. In short, she was disguised as a child who would not—when asked if the boys in her class got in trouble for a recent altercation involving a math book and a school toilet—reply, "No, they got to go to Disneyland to have the time of their lives."

Dick, my friend and fellow smart-mouth for these past 30 years, sees Rachael as the recipient of our smart-mouth legacy. "It's a worthless legacy," he said, "but it's the only one we have."

Not true. Being as we are a half-Catholic family, I can (from my half) also pass on things like first Communion.

"I did this same thing. And your ancestors did this same thing going back a thousand years," I told Rachael, as she tried to pin the flower crown to her permanently messy hair.

"How did you look in flowers?" she asked.

Actually, we boys wore white suits—jacket, pants, shirt and tie, all white. We looked like Rose Parade officials. And from that day until we outgrew the stupid outfits, our mothers spent much of their time trying to get us to wear them a second time.

Surprisingly, the kid enjoys the pomp. And the pomp is never better than during one of the major sacraments. On Saturday we had your seven priests in vestments, candles, crosses, flowers, stained glass and 80 kids in white (boys in shirt and tie, no jackets) with hands folded and heads lowered as they walked piously past their parents' video and still cameras.

There were fewer cameras on hand for the Nixon funeral.

And there were no less than 35 people waiting when we arrived home, 35 people who consumed six dozen rolls, a case of champagne, three 10-pound smoked turkeys and enough smooshy salad to float the Mary Kate from Memphis to New Orleans.

Everyone brought their children, who mixed and moved through the day's alternating shadow and sun like whirlwinds self-adjusted by age and interests.

At one point, 11-year-old Ethan (the Ultimate Boy) was cut from a pack of ball players and paraded before me.

"Look," my 11-year-old daughter said, grabbing the tiny gold earring hanging from a hole in his ear. "Does this seem suddenly unfair?"

Indeed it did. For I have put off her ear-piercing until the age of 14.

Why? I don't know why. Fourteen seemed like a good age. That's all.

"I just changed my mind," I said. "You don't even have to check with your mother."

But I didn't change my mind on all this other stuff, on the ceremony and the children all dressed in white and the priests like something out of the Middle Ages and all these grown-ups who dedicated a Saturday to a little kid with missing teeth because that's what we do from time to time.

For that, there must be great blessings due from somewhere.

A call in the night lets a grown son know he's an orphan

July 26, 1994

The phone rang at midnight. It would have been far more dramatic if I had been asleep, but I wasn't. The moonlight in the room was too strong, and I was already fighting the Monday morning blues.

Besides, I knew what it was. I even knew who would be on the line. I've known it on a conscious level for a year or more. A woman gets into her late 70s and starts failing in small increments with an unending series of strokes, and we all know where that's going.

So it wasn't a tragedy in the usual sense coming down the phone lines. My mother was not, after all, a child or someone with big things ahead of her or behind her. She was just a woman who did what she was supposed to do, which, looking backward from this wretched time, makes her seem damned heroic.

Then again, maybe that's not completely true. There was not then, nor is there now, a shortage of women abandoned with children, women who work the jobs and put up the good fight out of love and something that goes beyond love. In the animal world, it's the same reflex that makes it so dangerous to stand between a female anything and her babies.

In our case, it was protection you couldn't buy, and warmth. It was love with Old World origins, heartfelt and uneducated, a love sunk to the neck in passion and it stood between us and a lot of rotten stuff until something as simple and enormously complex as broken blood vessels in the brain took it away.

In the end, she didn't know us. She had her vocabulary and her body, but her memory, if it was there at all, was submerged. Still, even before she went into full-erase, she was happy about our expecting a baby boy and even more excited when he arrived, she had an Old Country thing about baby boys.

Then the darkness descended, and my sisters were left to move her to a place where she could be cared for by people used to the mood swings that come to those fortunate enough to live long lives and unfortunate enough to not be rewarded with dying outright.

So I have expected this call, expected it even more so lately when the dreams began, virtual-reality dreams where I would open our bedroom door in the night and surprise my mother as she ducked into the room shared by our daughters.

It's so melodramatic, but I'd open the door and there she'd be in the same bright red—we're talking Italian-bright here—party dress going to see her girls.

Last night I didn't have the dream. I had the phone call.

It was my sister. She was crying, telling me mom had passed away.

That's the term she used, passed away—words that don't exist in the journalistic vocabulary. In newspapers, people die; they don't pass away, pass on, pass to the other side or go to their reward. They die and are survived by children, grandchildren and great-grandchildren. We allow that, their names and numbers, because they are a kind of obituary code that speaks about family or the vision of family that will be tucked into the prayer books for all time to come.

The dead in the obits are beloved or greatly missed. Not being completely cold, we allow slightly bigger cliches as the deceased's age descends toward childhood.

When you're near 80, death isn't a tragedy. Nor is it unexpected. It just happens, like the inevitable falling of the front ranks in battle. One row down, next row on deck. It's often likened to a circle, but it's more a shooting gallery taking all of us in turn.

Yesterday we were beloved children; today we are orphans.

I, suddenly and belatedly, have no father or mother.

But we are parents with small ones who search our faces for cracks. We are the rock upon which their fragile house is built. They alone know this. If the order holds, they alone will remember—as the children of Rose Bogert remember—and recall the love.

Nothing is as chaotic as dad and kids home alone

October 18, 1994

If I had any knowledge of higher mathematics I'd be able to compute the odds of having a child and a dog take sick, having two book reports and two jog-a-thon sponsor sheets suddenly come due and facing an unhappy pair of police officers in my boxer shorts all within hours of my wife leaving for a conference in Temecula.

Temecula, she said, is near San Diego. So, relatively speaking, is Brazil. Not that I was thinking about this as the dear woman explained the vagaries of running the household in her absence.

Sure, sure, yes dear, no dear, of course dear.

It's not good to be too smug because life has a way of turning on you. As it did the moment my wife walked out the door making bye-bye motions to a baby whose little nose immediately began running until—within five minutes—he looked like Henry VIII on a bender.

Of course, it was then 5 p.m., after doctor hours and a prime moment for my two daughters to produce their empty jog-a-thon sheets and announce the book reports.

"It's no big deal," said one, "we have all the way until tomorrow morning at 6."

"Snort, sneeze, sniffle!" said the baby.

"What's for dinner?" asked another.

That was an odd question because their mother had just said something about the freezer and turning the oven, I think it was, to 425 degrees and making sure they got vegetables.

"Let's order pizza!" I suggested, delivered pizza being the only real proof that God exists.

The jog-a-thon problem was just as easy to solve. Like most things in life, it required the cleaning out of my pitiful checkbook and wallet to cover donations by made-up sponsors that were never found.

This, of course, meant the children would have to pay for the pizza. Which they agreed to do after I signed an IOU. They don't trust the repayment plan devised by my mother, a plan where you borrow money from your kids then, when they ask for repayment, you say "Who puts a roof over your head?"

They made me sign. And the doctor, when I got her on the phone, recommended an assortment of medications for the baby that required a trip to the drugstore and use of a credit card because I didn't want to sign another IOU to my kids, who have cash wads like Mafia capos.

On our return we found our sheeplike dog gone violently sick after eating leftover pizza and the cardboard carton it came in.

Barf-a-rama, but nothing compared to report writing among the yammering youths and a blessed desert-like silence that followed and lasted until 2 a.m. when the baby awoke wet, hungry and clogged like a bad drain.

So I changed him, fed him and carried him into our breakfast room, where his screams set off the alarm sensor that detects the sound of breaking glass and eardrums—WAHWAHWAHWAHWAHWAH!

And that was just the kid. The alarm was even louder. It brought out the dogs and the girls who wanted to watch me fight a burglar. We turned it off and waited for the alarm company to call. But they didn't because (they claimed) our line was busy. That's why they called the police.

Have you ever wondered how they get so many bright lights and barking radios on one squad car? And they were all on, with a grim policewoman at the door, looking me up and down, looking at the dogs, the children, me in boxer shorts and a Sesame Street T-shirt explaining like a mental patient how all this came to pass while a another officer stood behind a tree (seriously) looking edgy.

And all the time I'm waiting for my 8-year-old to say, "He kidnapped us!" But she doesn't and after a moment the officer says that false alarms cost the city money.

Then she leaves me, the drag on society, holding my clogged baby and wondering if Temecula was too long a drive and how we'd be met.

Parents develop attention deficit the third time around

November 11, 1994

One thing is certain about raising children: The second child doesn't get near the attention the first did. While the third—three being the number needed to say that you have "children"—gets . . . hey, where is that kid?

Excuse me.

"Has anybody seen the baby!" Oh, there he is, eating a plant.

As I was saying, the first baby gets treated like Prince Charles at Vons with cameras banging away constantly, with relatives asking for locks of hair and folk jetting in just to gaze upon her.

This is funny in retrospect, especially the retrospect provided by the crate of photos you own of that first child, photos that prove that she was nowhere near as perfect as you thought. In fact, seen from a distance of 12 years, that first baby looks pretty much like all babies—fat-cheeked, slobbering, diapered. If you woke up looking like that, you'd run to the plastic surgeon.

Then comes baby two with its deja vu. "We have," you say, "already done this." The entire endeavor has, as all things must, palled. Yet, despite your love of this runner-up, you are not easily moved to bringing out the camera.

Excuse me again. "Has anybody seen the baby?"

Fine. He's with his sisters in a roomful of dangerous objects. Not to worry. Now, where was I? Oh, yes, baby three. We had this one a year ago. In fact, my wife called at 12:23 on the momentous afternoon to congratulate me.

"Congratulations for what?" I asked.

"Your son was born a year ago this very minute," she said, sounding crestfallen. Still, that was interesting. If he were born one year ago, that would make this his birthday.

"Wait. Are we supposed to get him something?" I asked, not meaning to sound callous. But we should face this fact about 1-year-olds: They don't know their birthday from Shinola. It's like dressing the kid in a cute little lion costume and taking him out trick-or-treating. People went nuts, fondling his little lion ears, grabbing his little lion tail and heaping his bag with candy.

During this entire process, the kid was like someone on leave from a Martian jungle. He had no idea. But he went along anyway, good sport. And he only had the lion costume, I should add, because both his sisters wore it before him. See what I mean about third children?

"Get him something for his birthday, will you?" my wife asked.

Why not? Toys R Us is close by The Breeze R Us and full of games and balls for all seasons. But what was I thinking as I prowled the well-stocked aisles? I was thinking that we already have a houseful of like-new toys.

Take the vast Barbie doll collection. Why can't we recycle them? Yes, that's the environmentally sound word I'm looking for; we could recycle by cutting their long hair, spray painting them camouflage green and renaming them Mutant GI Ninja Barbie Joe. The kid will never know.

But my wife would, so I went with wooden blocks and one of those moronic pole things you slip bright plastic rings over. It was a low-end buy but far more generous than my daughters, who took the 20 bucks I gave them to a toy store and came away with a $3 toy for bro and two $7 gifts for themselves.

On the way home, still in a giving mood, I stopped at Ralphs to buy a cake. Only they didn't have any. So I bought a frozen pumpkin pie figuring he could, because it's mushy, eat that and because that's the first thing I saw. C'mon, like the kid really knows! Besides, he enjoyed it, jamming big globs of the stuff into his mouth at his party, where we all helped to blow out a single turkey-shaped candle borrowed from a Thanksgiving decoration.

Oh, yeah, I took a picture of him with all the dogs and sisters and friends of sisters. And know what? He was smiling like the happy boy he is.

Miscalculation lands him between rocks and a hard place

July 25, 1995

I relearned the meaning of hard work (as opposed to what I do for a living) on Saturday when the big dump truck backed up my driveway and the big tattooed driver climbed down.

"This can't be all mine?" I whined.

"You Bogert?" he asked, examining a clipboard like a star map. Yes. "Where you want them?"

"But I only ordered eight scoops."

"This is eight scoops. With the push-shoosh of a lever, they came to rest hugely at my feet, a pile of rocks the size of Connecticut.

"Mess!" said my 20-month-old son, who was—and this appears to be a boy trait—beside himself at the sight of a dump truck, a big hairy tattooed guy and a large pile of gravel in his driveway. Face it, when you're 20 months old, everything looks like a UFO.

"Little boys like this stuff," said the driver who, it turns out, has a small son of his own. "Only my son doesn't wear pink barrettes in his hair," he pointed out.

Now that he mentioned it, the boy was indeed wearing pink barrettes in his hair—two of them, one for each of the sisters who put them there. And he looked kind of sweet.

"Who's going to help you move all this?"

"Them," I said, pointing to my two daughters (the hairdressers, 12 and 8) and Matthew (also 8) from next door.

"Going to get killer-hot soon," he said, driving off to further adventures in delivery, leaving me to question what I might have been thinking when I asked the woman at the stone yard how much gravel I needed to cover 500 square feet of dog run.

"Five scoops," she replied—scoops apparently being the way gravel people measure things. For example, one might ask, "How many scoops of time till lunch?" or "I love you 100 scoops!"

"Give me eight," I replied.

She gazed at me over the tops of her glasses. "Anything you say, Diamond Jim. By the way, that's way too much."

Well, there it was, way too much. And it all had to be scooped into a wheelbarrow and moved 30 feet across bumpy ground to what used to be a wonderful grassy area until our two dogs ground it into something resembling Mogadishu.

"Don't worry," my 8-year-old said. "You have us."

I did have them, by God, along with the sun and—within an hour—I didn't even have them in a meaningful way. Soon my meticulous 12-year-old was meticulously arranging the gravel I had moved into Zen-garden swoops and curls while the two 8-year-olds were arguing: "Shut up! "No, you shut up!"

Meanwhile, I'm heat-hallucinating my beautiful wife's cool slim figure by the enormous gravel pile. Moving closer, T-shirt wrapped around my head for sun protection, I see that it is my wife and she is angry.

"Our cars," she said, "are on the other side of this stuff."

"The good news," I said, trying to be cheery in the face of physical and mental collapse, "is that the cars can't be stolen. The bad news is, the cars also cannot be driven."

Suddenly, the effort went from just moving stones in oppressive heat to clearing a path for a car. It was the winter of 1958 all over again and a swath had to be cut through snow. Next to gravel, there is nothing more futile than shoveling what is essentially water.

And this I did. I sweated water and shoveled rock. At one point my 8-year-old looked upon the heat-hazed mess and, Omar Sharif-like, proclaimed, "They call it the Devil's anvil!"

This while our two massive dogs—the very beasts that caused me to buy two tons of gravel—slept wet-nose-to-wet-nose on a couch in an air-conditioned house dreaming the dreams of the smartest race on earth.

Sympathize with Fuhrman? Next racial target could be you

August 31, 1995

I'll tell you this from experience. There are some people who are going to agree with O.J. investigator Mark Fuhrman, men and women who are going to gut-react well to his brutal instant-justice philosophy because the world he inhabited as an L.A. cop is not (as he put it) all patty cakes.

You think the punks, the yos, the Rolling 69 Gangsta Crips are kidding around with the automatic weapons, with the blood in their eyes?

If you think that, you're the patty cake. You're saying guys like Fuhrman—and all the men and women who aren't at all like Fuhrman but are nonetheless being paid to face these city creeps off—are paranoid, alarmist.

Like you aren't riding around with your doors locked. Like mentioning that you're going jewelry shopping up on Spring Street or that you've visited Watts Towers doesn't bring gasps from the white folks, Asian folks, Latinos or African-Americans who don't have to live near these places.

It's a class thing. If you're out of the hardness and squalor, you're out and it doesn't much matter what color you are. Taking care of all that is someone else's business, cop business.

Let them go into the projects wearing six-shooters and body armor, let them pull the carloads of young males over and wonder if they might be leaving the scene in a body bag.

Any way you look at it, it's a mean, lousy job. Lucky for us, lots of people are willing to do it out of a sense of duty, out of what a Torrance cop once told me was a built-in sense of justice.

He said: "They see wrong, they want to fix it."

And Dirty Harry, the guy everyone is conjuring up as the semi-coherent Fuhrman tapes play out, isn't the only cop who detests the ACLU and what it represents and the ACLU and what it doesn't represent.

But what the hell, it's all about liberal attitudes that let killers walk. Liberals, it's obvious, are in favor of accepting the Twinkie defense, or the deprived-childhood defense, or the mean-smacking-daddy defense or the yo-mama defense as reason enough to kill children or knock over 7-Elevens.

So it is against this perception of permissiveness and in favor of rare lone-stars like Fuhrman that will trigger an instant moral alignment in some, a favorable reading of "Nigger driving a Porsche that doesn't look like he's got a $300 suit on, you always stop him" or "How do you intellectualize when you punch the hell out of a nigger? He either deserves it or he doesn't."

And that's the trouble here, the giant fall-down, the words that would make Dirty Harry himself say, "Hold on, buddy."

Fact of the matter is, this is America and we're all niggers, dagos, micks, spics, kikes, slants or some damn thing, and nearly every one of us is willing to point that out from time to time. Even those who flee to Idaho or some other white dream world like to turn around and tell visiting reporters how they're just happy as hell to be away from all the colored weirdness.

That's what I mean when I say that some people won't see what all the fuss is about ex-detective Fuhrman's honest statements. This lying sack of dung—if he wasn't just talking big for a cracker college teacher with cop movie dreams—was hitting the racial nail squarely on the head.

But what, one has to ask, if the nigger turns out to be me?

I know, sometimes you just have to worry about his brand of street justice later. Or maybe we don't worry later because we don't know what to know or care.

But we should care, down to the bottom of our little racist, quasi-racist or just mildly irritated-by-people-who-ain't-like-us souls because there is no justifying or stopping this world-destroying disease, no way to say it isn't you who's the nigger next time.

Sharing in a boy's rite of passage

September 10, 1995

This happened a decade ago while walking my curly haired 3-year-old daughter up our street. It was our break-in walk: new house, new neighborhood and (would you look) a little boy your own age!

Of course, being kids of their age, the little boy stared at my little girl who stared right back. Neither spoke. Nor did they smile.

"That was Brian Schaefer," she announced much later.

"So why didn't you say hello?" I asked.

"Didn't want to," she replied, adding this completely nutty note about the composition of her preschool class: "We have three Brian Schaefers in our room."

Well, there weren't three Brians. There was only this one, and he lived up our street. And soon they were thick-or-thin best friends in a way one rarely sees between boys and girls. What's more, they have remained friends through all the trick-or-treating, through hours of movies, books, coloring, swimming and talking like that other rare commodity, brothers and sisters who love one another.

In a way, Brian became our son. The son we thought we'd never have, but eventually did, which makes him a first son. And his parents, Denise and Jim, and their extended family became our friends. Maybe best of all, Brian and his family gave our little girl their religion, Judaism.

God knows, in a religious household like theirs, this was standing convention on its head. But Brian and Caitlin were friends and Brian just couldn't have Shabbas (Sabbath) dinner on Friday evening without her.

And Caitlin, ever one to be included, couldn't have Shabbas if Brian and his brothers wore yarmulkes and she didn't. So they bought her one, in her favorite color (pink) and they let her take part.

She drank it in, Shabbas on Friday and church on Sunday like the greatest story ever told, which it is. Then came the wonderfully religiously confused night that she suddenly blurted "What day is this?" Friday. "Friday. It's Shabbas!"

"That's OK," I said. "You're Catholic."

"Oh, yeah," she said.

But the kid is also and forever a little bit Jewish—maybe a lot Jewish—in the same way that Brian is a little bit our boy. And here he was on this fine Saturday morning becoming a man. OK, maybe the manhood thing was a little difficult to believe.

This, after all, was half of the duo who only a few years ago believed me when I told them that their cannonballing into the pool caused all the water to rise into the air and settle back down just in time to catch them.

This is the kid who once sat on our kitchen counter eating pancakes, the kid who'd walk our little girl home when they were both 4 and heartbreakingly cute to make sure she arrived safely, the kid who always brought presents from vacation and sent birthday cards.

This was our Brian, the sweet boy who still keeps us buying Kosher hot dogs just in case, the kid who is always polite, sweet, considerate toward younger children, smart, funny and quite extroverted.

That was him at temple running his bar mitzvah like a talk show host, introducing his family and friends with ease and in a voice that was at once boyish and (what the heck, yes) manly.

That was him reading beautifully in Hebrew and reminding us how little boys and little girls just like this have helped keep this ancient language and religion (the religion that gave the world Christianity, the Old Testament, Jesus and Brian) in temples like this through shattering centuries of misery, misunderstanding and murder.

At one point in the long service, Brian was handed the Torah on its great wooden spools. From the hands of his grandparents to the hands of his parents to Brian, the ancient weight of history, salvation, law and suffering—the history of a great and tenacious people—passed.

Me, I was the sap standing misty-eyed as this newly minted man passed by with the matchless text cradled in his arms. Shabbat shalom, Brian Schaefer.

It was a gift come forward from the old ones, a gift to question and cherish but a gift nonetheless and a miracle—every bit of it.

Many more than a million men need to learn responsibility

October 17, 1995

Monday's Million Man March brought the old man to his feet, stood him up like a shooting gallery duck—a dead duck and unknowable.

No calling George up and playing tough guy, no asking why—during 22 years of marriage to my mother—he was never there with the paycheck, never there at all unless he was drunk and up to some face punching.

Over time I tried to make sense of a man who spent his life in whiskey bars and at the track. I'd ask my older sisters, and they'd say, "There's nothing to make sense of."

What I do know is this: Just before my eldest sister's 15th birthday, she walked into our daddy-wretched home and told my mother, "Either he goes or I go."

Here's how my mother reacted: "Good idea." And together daughter and mother gathered up father/husband's belongings and placed them on the other side of the locked door that he would come to pound upon and bellow at until he left more or less forever.

Here's what I remember: I'm maybe 6 years old and standing on our front porch when my father drives past in one of those whale-shaped cars of the early 1950s. Laughing, he points not at me but at our house as he goes. He is pointing for the woman who is tucked under his right arm.

When I told my mother (in what was to become a family joke), she replied, "Where did he get a car?"

The women, I later learned, were constant. Why my mother took it was another matter. It was a different time, she was dependent, she was a devout Roman Catholic, she was as abused and beaten down as a POW.

Times change, the reasons for enduring do not.

A few years after finding his junk in the hallway, my father gave all three of us over to my mother's new husband in adoption. Widowed, with no children of his own and already past 50, this stranger would become our real father.

But he wasn't an eraser. Our father didn't vanish. He would show up sometimes—after Saratoga and just before Gulf Stream—to say hello.

Sometimes he'd take me out with one of his companions, women who smoked, wore heavy face powder and couldn't have been nicer to me in their boozy lost ways.

By the age of 10, I was calling my biological father George and a complete stranger Dad because one plainly deserved it and the other did not. One man did what he was supposed to do and the other did not.

All this, of course, is the Million Man March and the 3 billion-man march. It's about men who—like perpetual boys—need to be reminded perpetually of life's rules.

Statistically speaking, being the son of divorce gives me a 50 percent greater chance of the same. Or it might had I not also been granted a good stepfather and a tank corps of sturdy Old World uncles whose lives were defined from the family outward.

One should hesitate to claim such resolve in a young child. But what I have always wanted, from age 6 onward—from that day on the porch onward—was the opposite of what I saw in that passing car.

Still, the mystery of what I saw remains like the ghost smell of cigarettes. Driven by the overblown regard even grown children have for parents, I continue to think about this man and the devil that left him—in the end—alone in a distant hospital room consumed by all that he had consumed, calling his eldest daughter and getting his only son by chance.

"John, is that you?" he asked, surprised, delighted, near death, a frightened, burned-out man finally, needing his boy. "Johnny, it's you."

"I'll get my sister."

Those were my last and only words.

Even sweet-faced little boys sometimes find it hard to share

October 22, 1995

For years and years I had only daughters and liked it. Daughters are wild and nice when they're little and tend to go all mysterious and female as they grow, with the exception of my 9-year-old Rachael, who is as mysterious as a freight train.

Then we had this little boy who is, for a father of two daughters, weird.

"It's a boy," I recall the doctor saying as she bombarded our unborn child with ultrasonic rays.

"You can't be sure," I replied, allowing what I knew about these video blurs (they can't be sure) to tamper with what I was clearly seeing.

"That ain't his thumb," the doctor said, rather indelicately pointing out the kid's Johnson.

And nothing has been the same since. For starters, there was the boy thing. I didn't know how I'd react to a boy. Could I, for instance, hug a boy?

I mean, we're both guys, right?

The answer from the moment he arrived, like a warm loaf of bread with eyes, was clear. I could. Then we set about treating him like just another member of the family who happens to be extremely dangerous to himself and others.

Then there's the matter of girls. He likes girls. And maybe it's only me who sees the leering face of Jack Nicholson in his angelic smile.

And what about all the joyful head-butting and happy throat-grabbing, the playful attacks with plastic bats and the way he goes completely nutty over trucks, heavy equipment and cars.

"Car, car, car!" he shouts on the freeway. To this, one of his sisters will reply, "Imagine, Ian spotted a car, in Los Angeles!"

Then comes a recent Saturday evening and Adam, who is only a day younger than our Ian and—we incorrectly figured—a perfect match for some frenetic 2-year-old boy-centered play.

"Hey! Look, Ian, here's Adam!" we enthused parent-like when Adam arrived.

"Hey, Adam!" waxed Adam's parents. "Here's Ian!"

The rest was disaster, with Ian dedicating the entire evening to keeping Adam away from his stuff in a god-awful display of maleness never before witnessed in our once all-female household.

"Mine!" said sweet-faced little Ian, grabbing every toy the equally sweet-faced little Adam picked up. "Mine! You dog!"

OK, so he didn't say "You dog," but the implication was there as Ian protected the massive existing infrastructure of toys inherited from his older sisters. Even with the Barbies taken out, we're talking a plethora here, an Everest, a junkyard of abused playthings, most of which Ian never plays with, none of which he was willing to share.

It was like watching "Wild Kingdom." All the dreadful scene needed was the Marlin Perkins voice-over: "Notice how Ian puffs himself up and stands way too close to the intruding male. Notice how he eyeballs the visitor, how he wrestles the wooden truck from him, how he yanks away the basketball and the Mickey Mouse magic wand and how, like the lion of the forest, Mutual of Omaha safeguards your family's future. . ."

Wait! Sorry. I got carried away with old Marlin.

God, was this upsetting, especially when Adam innocently entered Ian's plastic Fun Time Happy House and Ian charged like a rhino. Right through the happy plastic door he went to grab Adam and chuck him out, rug-burning him into the carpet.

"My house. You dog," he said, as we screamed in what might as well have been Serbo-Croatian—"Ian! You have to share!"

Luckily, Adam's father laughed. That's because every day he takes Adam to day care and every day little sweet-faced Adam (with the eyelashes to die for) takes what he wants from anyone smaller than him with these words, "Mine! You dog!"

"Adam," his dad laughed, "you finally got your butt kicked."

What can I say, it kind of made sense.

Parents take note of their daughter's assets and liabilities

October 26, 1995

I was looking up the chimney the other day. Wait. Let me explain. On second thought, I don't have to explain anything. Besides, my wife was making me do this. She wants a gas log.

God, I hate gas logs. So it's too bad that I also hate hauling in real logs and hauling out their remains.

Anyway, I'm looking up the chimney, which is a fairly silly thing to do because it's flashlight-eating dark up there, dirty dark except for the note. Yes, a note, which would surprise anyone but me. That's because I'm Rachael's father, Rachael being our 9-year-old backup daughter, Rachael being someone who writes notes that can be found just about anywhere, even up chimneys.

It began, "Dear Santa, I know this is early so I hope you don't mind . . ."

Well, of course Santa doesn't mind. Neither do I. What do I have anyway?—maybe a year more of this Santa stuff before she starts acting like her older sister with the cool look of someone who knows how to fashion a thermonuclear device out of common household objects.

Rachael continued, "Here's what I'd like for Christmas if you have enough of these things. If you don't, that's

OK because I already have a lot of stuff; 1.) A new black bike because I hate riding the one with pink tires and the Cabbage Patch Kid front basket that belonged to my sister; 2.) A Dr. Dreadful Food and Drink Laboratory P.S. You forgot to give it to me last year but that's OK too; 3.) A collectors house."

(Parent's note: She didn't get a Dr. Dreadful Food Laboratory last year because I had no idea what it was. Ditto for the "collectors house" and the black bike because the Cabbage Patch bike is still perfectly good.)

"4.) A pair of black hietops (note: you get the idea); 5.) A mirror and a thermometer for Fang's aquarium."

Fang, by the way, is Rachael's gopher snake. It lives in her room and eats one live mouse per week. Except for the highly allegorical mouse-consuming business—meant to teach small children that the world is a place of senseless death—he's the best pet we've ever had. And he apparently needs a mirror, which is odd considering that snakes are practically blind, and a thermometer so (I'm only guessing here) he'll know what to wear on any given day.

The list continues: "7.) New collars for Cymbre and Clifford (they are dogs, ha!), rawhide bones, and big sleeping pillows with their names on them or with their names not on them; 8.) A bird in a cage. Thanks, Rachael. P.S.—I'll leave a McDonald's gift certificate and a free pass to any Mann Theater for a movie."

Yes, this is nearly as charming a note as the one she left us after last week's command appearance before her fourth-grade teacher, a woman who is about as amused by Rachael as one can be for what they pay her.

"She needs to pay more attention to her basic math facts," her teacher told us as we sat folded into these tiny desks. She added, "Rachael also needs to be less dramatic. That's the exact word she used, "dramatic."

Then she told us that every teacher in the school has

their own favorite Rachael story. They find her "unique," a word that can mean so much more than what it sounds like. They also fully expect to some day see her on television speeding around in a Zodiac boat, putting herself between whales and exploding Japanese harpoons.

We later explained all this (all but the whale business, why give her ideas?) to the kid in an exchange that seemed fruitful until we found the following note on our bed.

On it were two columns. Under the one marked "Good things about Rachael" were listed "Likes animals, especially whales, even insects; friendly, likes jokes, never plays with Barbies." Under the column marked "Bad things about Rachael" there was one entry, "Hates math," followed by a P.S. "Sue me."

It could all be genetic.

An admired friend is gone, but the grand old memories live on

January 7, 1996

Talking to Lynn last weekend I asked, "How are you doing?"

"Fine, for somebody dying," he replied across the long lines from South Florida.

William Lynn Boling was dying fast of liver failure, and it was like something playing out in another world. Death from a great distance grants us that illusion like those guys looking down from the Enola Gay.

Only Lynn's voice was still his own—weak but smart and strongly suggesting that I hadn't changed much since I was 13, a geek and his brother Dick's best friend.

"When's the Fiesta Bowl anyway?" I asked, bringing an ancient joke to a University of Georgia man who never missed the chance to remind me when my rival Florida Gators were doing badly.

"Tuesday," he said and all I'm thinking of is a day in September 1963 when Lynn and this entire country were on a roll. Only two years older than Dick and me, Lynn was the gifted one, the blessed one.

Lynn was a risk-taker. Lynn was a golden All-American swimmer. Lynn was a senior and drove a monster Pontiac Grand Prix when we were sophomores on bicycles. Girls loved Lynn. He was a little dangerous. There also was something courtly and Southern in him that he had carried away from his native Louisiana. Lynn treated us like Eddie Haskel treated the Beaver.

Even when the equation changed, when Lynn went off to college and came back nicer, driving a blood-red 'Vette and married to a matchlessly beautiful woman, working summers as a beach lifeguard with his own pad—even after we all grew up and reality set in, components of that respect remained.

Dick and I talked about that during the week, about how we never quite got over the fact that Lynn remained the immortal big brother.

He always seemed grown-up. When we were college hippies, he was in Atlanta putting together real estate deals and actually buying a beautiful old home while the rest of us were wondering if owning more than one pair of jeans might seem too capitalist.

Lynn lived fast. Lynn had beautiful wives and drove treacherously expensive automobiles and he did better financially than I could ever dream until the real estate bubble burst, and it all came crashing down, bringing far too much of the old Lynn down with it.

Through it all there was Lynn the gentleman, the guy who'd prepare a gourmet dinner for you when you came to town, the tough guy who would show you the delicate orchids growing on his patio.

That was the man, or what you could see of the man, who remained—even after his fall from grace, even after life turned in on him—loved.

I saw Lynn last year in a hangout fish joint down in Fort Lauderdale. My wife asked if that wasn't him at the bar and I said yes. Only it was Lynn as he looked in high school—slender again, muscled, thick-haired, unmistakably him; smiling, drawling, "Bogert, where'd your hair go?" Then, "Hell, you look better like this."

So we talked, and it turned out that his partner for the evening was the same person he took to his senior prom, the same girl he was sitting with in the front seat of his dad's brand-new Lincoln Continental when Scott Aaron's pet spider monkey got loose from a neighboring yard and jumped screaming out of a coconut palm onto the car's hood.

He told the story that night in the same way he explained it to his father, the now departed and grand old gentleman who said, "Lynn, come see me when you're ready to tell the truth."

Then comes the call and me stumbling, telling him how much I always liked him and how damn sorry I was that all this was happening and asking what I could do. And Lynn, depleted and 48 hours from death, said "Chant for me."

Or cry for him, our lost brother.

A child might grow up, but it seems his parents just get older

January 28, 1996

This is probably a strange way to look at a kid's life. Still, our 2-year-old, Ian, was born to a 45-year-old father, which means I will be 50 when he is 5 and 65 when he is 20.

In between, there will come, if we're lucky, grand moments when we will work on cars and toss balls back and forth—lots of ball-throwing in our future, I can tell already, and the fighting with plastic swords.

Still, he's the walking clock his sisters aren't. That's because I can't recall, not without subtracting and probably being off by at least a year, how old I was when either of them were born. That's because I was younger and did not yet think as I now do.

In fact, I did not begin to think like a time bomb until Ian came along which, as I said, happened a month after I turned 45. So, it is a confluence of the two events—my age and his appearance in the vast snake-river of time—that has turned him into a little yammering clock.

All of which tends to make me highly aware of him and of what he thinks and feels. There has lately been way too much evidence of both in his developing speech, which is itself a miracle.

But there should be no surprises here. Two children came before him. Still, we are surprised that he can do all the things he is supposed to do. I remember, just after our first kid arrived, watching my mother's near complete bafflement.

A woman who had raised four children on her own couldn't quite get the diaper right, couldn't recall when they start to speak, when potty training begins or when you rip the bottle out of their mouths.

I thought then that this was evidence of someone going soft when what we were seeing was pure mental preservation.

Here's how it works. One day you have no children. The next, after some months of clueless pregnancy, you own a baby—the original computer without a handbook. That's when you discover all the preparation hasn't prepared you for it in the least.

It's like watching the recent PBS "Frontline" on the Gulf War, where experienced commanders engaged enemy tanks for the first time and could only wonder open-mouthed, "So, this is the tank in battle!"

That was the warrior's wedding to the old knights, to men who trained and trained and couldn't know what it was really about until it happened.

On another terrifying level, that is what it's like to be a first-time parent with all the vomiting, illness and waking up uncomfortable and fearful.

And I'm just talking about the parents.

The baby is a whole other matter, and as foreign as war—something we remember as old soldiers remember combat. For them, it is camaraderie and good times. For parents, it is the images of parenthood depicted in ads from corporations trying to sell baby goods, ads in which dad is smiling and mom is a 19-year-old Swedish model.

We forget strategic portions of the early baby months like we forget being the target of artillery fire: It's all about mental survival.

So, we are surprised for a third time—or again for the third time—when baby talks, walks and points with grubby little fingers at a well-worn dinosaur book saying (in accordance with some master plan), “Terannarex!”

And we say to yet another child, “Know what T-Rex’s problem is?”

“Hungy!” the kid replies, baring sharp little mammal teeth.

So, we look forward to a third round of preschool, another first day of kindergarten, another teaching of multiplication tables, another discovery of America, another California mission project and the thought of attending PTA meetings in the year 2011.

Which is pronounced either “twenty-eleven” or “two-thousand-eleven,” which sound like science fiction to me.

His mission: building a better model

April 23, 1996

The kid, reading from her fourth-grade teacher's instructions, wanted to know: "Why did we choose for our project Mission San Gabriel Archangel?"

"Because," I replied, "it's miles closer than Mission Santa Barbara."

Why lie? That's what I did four years ago when I last helped a child over this educational hurdle. We lied about the mission's great beauty when, in reality, it was a quake-ravaged ruin in a lousy section of San Gabriel, and we lied about the treatment of the native Americans.

For this the teacher, who is years younger than me and tougher, lambasted us, saying we ignored the "downside" of the 225-year-old mission system.

The downside was slave labor and mass death by Euro-disease. In short, it was a long sad song never stressed for people of my generation, people whose formative years were spiced with movies about white cowboys taking target practice on native Americans.

This time we included the really depressing facts. Yet this, as parents of many fourth-graders know, is not the difficult part. Face it, most of us can write. It's the mission model that's the killer.

I'm talking about normal men and women going suddenly anxiety riddled because we, plainly, are not our fathers. We do not own work benches, table saws and a wall of nicely hung tools. That's because our dads and moms worked really hard to send us to colleges, where we learned really useful things like iambic pentameter.

I've been running into these overly educated, mechanically challenged losers for weeks.

"So," they ask, eyes nervously casting about, "how's that mission project coming?"

"OK," I'd reply, hiding the fact that I alone had the supreme foresight to hide our last mission project under a tarp in the garage for four long years just so I could rip the cover back and proclaim "Voila. Behold the . . . completely wrecked mission project."

"It hasn't improved with age," the fourth-grader said, adding "and it looks like a mouse has been living in it."

Closer examination revealed that a mouse had indeed been living in the wood and board creation but had long since abandoned it. Which says pretty much everything we need to know about the general condition of something that its previous owner—on one of her infrequent pass-bys of our work area—deemed "not all that good to begin with."

Lacking alternatives, we went to work cleaning, rebuilding, laying new fake grass and adding new bells to a tower omitted from the original model due to lack of interest on the builder's part.

In all, it took 11 hours before the kid said, "You know, it doesn't look all that bad if you squint when you look at it." She considered adding a "please squint" sign to the model's plywood base but figured it might clash with our ace-in-the hole, our genuine piece of original mission adobe taken from among many historically significant McDonald's wrappers in a genuine mission dumpster filled during renovations that have transformed the old church.

Anyway, we labeled it "genuine adobe." And we weren't feeling all that bad about our labors until we brought it to school Monday morning and saw that we had produced a mission only marginally better than one built of sugar cubes.

One wretched boy had an absolutely perfect rendering of our same mission down to arcades, arches, graves, wells and little tonsured scale-model monks loafing about the grounds.

"How'd you do this, punk?" I asked its little punk owner.

"My dad's an architect," the punk replied, pride oozing from between his teeth along with bits of the Ding-Dong he was eating.

And all the other models of absolute perfection. Where did they come from. Kits! You can now buy easy-to-assemble mission kits, any one you want. That's how things change in four years and how, in some backwaters, they stay just the same.

Memories from '50s explode

July 4, 1996

It began at South of the Border, in South Carolina to be precise, a place so kitschy that even I noticed. A kid raised in a pink stucco house, with a matching pink-flamingo-decorated screen door out front, actually noticed that this relentlessly advertised roadside souvenir stand just inside the state line was one huge example of poor taste.

Eisenhower was president, our Ford had fins like a ballistic missile and we were heading down to Florida for one of the vacations that would cause us to move there. The point of these pre-interstate bullet rides was, of course, getting there fast. Dad loved to get there, making time, passing up places of little importance (the Liberty Bell, Washington, D.C.) and saving precious moments out of our two-tone missile for important things.

You gotta stop at South of the Border, really. They urged us on, our fellow New Yorkers just returned from this yo-yo trip along the East Coast. It's so damn cute you'll scream—and me, all I could think about as I hung my head out the car window was what would happen if I bonked heads with a family dog traveling in the opposite direction.

Anyway, my parents' brain-dead friends believed that

making time on the East Coast somehow made them royalty. As proof that you did the grand tour and could afford a $6 motel room with a paper band on the toilet, you had to return home with a bug-flecked South of the Border bumper sticker.

They'd put one on your car for free while bored mortal kids plodded around behind parents who shopped bins of curios that ran toward the racist and the scatological. But what did they know. This was 1958, eight years removed from all manner of national turmoil and a federal ban on that Rolls-Royce of personal explosives, that legendary quarter-stick-O'-dy-no-mite, the M-80!

The good news, on the day I watched mom and pop price miniature outhouses, was that I was only minutes away from heaven.

I'm walking, looking down at ordinary Keds treading an ordinary world. Then I look up. Only the world had changed like Cortes coming out of the jungle and into Tenochtitlan.

In front of me was a vision grander than the Seven Cities, greater still than the Vatican, more magnificent than the tombs of Luxor. And it was all done up in cellophane wrappings of red, white and blue.

For South of the Border was then, and is now, the nation's largest fireworks retailer, a place where the most innocent item in stock was the garden-variety sparkler, which last year caused a mere 470 serious injuries.

They had M-80s! They had bright-red cherry bombs, 2-inchers, ashcans and explode-on-impact torpedoes like the one that would accidentally injure my right ear some years later in another hilarious Fourth of July accident.

Know what I did. I bought all I could in the name of fire, explosion, thunder, destruction, mayhem, mirth, murder and Gotterdammerung. For there exists, not so deeply buried in the little-boy soul, a need for these things.

This is why I bought and bought. Because I knew that these illegal fireworks would sell back home at prices driven by patriotism and the aforementioned desire of little boys to carry a string of 1-inch firecrackers in their socks. This not so much for the lighting but for the sheer boundless joy of holding something lethal so close to bare flesh.

Only our later sexual awakening would equal the pleasure then associated with the sound of black powder touched by flame. If some kid lost an eye or a finger to an M-80—which could turn a galvanized wash bucket into shrapnel—it was because he was a loser.

This was a combination of war and heaven, and July Fourth was its excuse. South of the Border, and lesser places catering to the same need, were its conduit. And the whole nasty routine has nearly vanished in these parts because all those nasty little boys grew up and became cops, firemen, trauma surgeons and (worse) parents, and the thought of explosives in the delicate hands of children came to scare the living hell out of them all.

But you can still hear it, right now this morning as you read—the distant pop-pop-pop like a chain gun in the middle-distance.

Now lie, old boy, and say it doesn't still call out to you.

Dogs connect man to his nature, roots and capacity for loving

March 23, 1997

It's a miserable August Saturday nine years ago and I'm in the pound killing time, waiting for my kid across the street in art class. I've also had a beer, which isn't the best thing to do in that kind of heat and might account for why the dogs on hand looked so ugly.

I'm talking torn-eared junkyard creatures out of hell except for this one shaggy, beige beast chasing his tail in the middle of his cage. He's maybe happy to find himself on death row and so deliriously happy to find a complete stranger staring at him that he flings all 100 pounds of his furry self at the chain link.

He's trying hard for a fence-lick. "You're a moron," I say. "And I don't like dogs."

The feeling, obviously, isn't mutual. Later, I tell my wife, "There was this idiot sheep-like dog at the pound, only he's beige."

The next week the kid's in art class and I'm back at the pound restating the obvious to the still bottomlessly happy beast: "You really are a moron." Only the real moron is me going back the next three Saturdays until a rubber-booted pound guy hauling a hose, and slicing a finger across his throat, says, "If you want that dog you better move quick."

An hour later I'm back with my wife and 2-year-old.

"That's the dog?" she asks, only now he's licking the kid's face. Then to the guy in the boots, "We'll take him."

The kid says, "He's a big good dog."

And so Clifford, fully grown and in possession of the only tricks he would ever know (sit, shake hands, speak) became our protector, sleeping nights beside our two girls and later—after the birth of our son—midway between their two rooms.

Clifford's only real fault was the way his natural affection for absolutely everyone got in the way of his sheep-like dog instincts. Cliff, named for the huge storybook dog, loved automatically. He loved the pirate crew that came to replace our roof, the homeless guy who appeared at our door and people I couldn't personally stand.

Still, he was a grand companion and—I figured going in—an object lesson. By watching the short arc of a dog's life, the theory goes, children learn about coping with love and loss. Anyway, that's what I believed because I had never owned a dog except for Buddy, a pound beast with poor bathroom habits that my parents tolerated for five days when I was 7.

In short, I didn't know the first thing about dogs. But I talked a great game as I did the washing, feeding, walking, running and getting slowly attached. I gave him those things and he gave me back a presence like a forest.

Ten-thousand years ago, Cliff's ancestors became the first animals to voluntarily surrender their wildness and cast their lot forever with man. This they did before cats and more completely than any creature.

They are ours, we are theirs and I'd say that I love this beast, but it's not love like I love any human. It's love for his linking me to nature and to what was once wild in both of us. That and his endless loyalty and how he is forever linked in mind with people I love. The moments come back, all usual—dog chasing child, child chasing dog, child dressing dog in jacket and pants, big dog not eating small child whole.

We weren't, of course, prepared for the shortness of his life-arc. While the children grew up, Clifford grew slowly old and arthritic in the spine. He lost weight, lost his drive, lost everything but his desire to stay with us. And it was a greatly diminished dog that I took to the vet last Wednesday after drugs and an ocean of little-kid hope failed to deliver up the crazy Clifford of old.

A miracle cure couldn't happen any more than an understanding of life's loss can be had on the cheap. He was 12 or maybe 13. His breathing is labored, he can't walk. And now we are in the examining room, his huge head in my lap, taking a junkie dream syringe as I speak into his ear the worst kind of nonsense—telling him how he changed us all and how he, Clifford, was just about the best good big dog ever.

Ex-sprinter, roped into coaching, sees kids' eagerness to run

March 26, 1998

"Maybe you could just come out and look at the sprinters," was the original request tendered by an 11-year-old absolutely beside herself because she goes to Catholic school and Catholic school doesn't guarantee that any team will exist unless some sucker comes forward to coach it.

You see, there wasn't supposed to be a track team this year at my kid's school because the former volunteer coach's last kid graduated and she no longer needed the parent volunteer hours (again, Catholic school) or the headache of turning a bunch of fifth- through eighth-graders into something resembling trained runners.

"I hear you're going to coach our sprinters!" came the voice of a grown man across the phone lines not an hour later, a grown man who had been conned into a time-chewing job vacated by a wised-up mom with a real P.E.

degree. "I was a distance man myself, so an old sprinter could really help."

My kid was sort of dancing right there beside me begging as the trap closed: "Just take a look."

Only taking a look required being on the track at 8 a.m. Saturday, just the old distance man and me making it clear that I was just there to offer a few suggestions.

"Coach Bogert," the old distance man announced out of nowhere, "will be working with you sprinters over there." Break. Wait, what's this coach stuff. And there I was surrounded by a flock of bright-faced boys and girls in retainers, gym shorts, inflatable basketball shoes and T-shirts with stuff like "I don't mind losing . . . I just don't want to be there" written on them. They also wore these expectant looks as if they were waiting for somebody to say something smart.

Finally one kid says, "What are we doing, coach?" It was my kid who asked.

"Well, I'm not actually a coach," I said. That's because a coach, in my experience, is a sadistic former Marine who makes small boys duckwalk around basketball courts while unfavorably comparing them to the real men he served with on Guadalcanal. A coach, more than anything, is someone who actually knows what he is doing.

"Coach?" This from another little kid whose feet looked like balloons on the ends of his skinny legs.

What are we talking about here, starts, curve running, baton passing. I only spent 10 years of my life doing these things in high school and college. What the heck. Let's do some starts before we go over to Starbucks.

So we hunkered down at the 100-meter line, nuzzled right up to the white stripe, fingers splayed directly under the shoulders, feet just so in the blocks, head down.

"Like an old fire horse," my kid remarks, and I guess it's true. Because 10 minutes out there brought it all back: the consuming desire, the hours at practice, the chronic injuries, then having to forget it all, leave it like a dead battery because there is nothing more pathetic than an old guy remembering. So I would not remember, not out loud anyway, because I had some small things to teach.

And they are eager to learn, or learn what they can in a sport where you mostly have it or mostly do not, the best thing being that they are at a time in life where it doesn't mean a thing if they beat or are beaten as long as they enjoy the matchless high of it.

You can make them faster at the start and in the turns, in the hand-offs. There is time to be made in the rudiments: the don't look back, the don't let up or give in, aiming for that imaginary line 10 yards beyond the tape.

The rest nobody has to teach. Kids have heart as standard equipment. They like to run until you have to haul them back in yelling, never revealing the central mystery of the sprint—which is, no matter how fast you are, you will always fear the undiscovered fast kid, the boy or girl with the bigger gift who is at that moment smoking Lucky Strikes out behind the A&W.

"What now?" a boy asks, antsy, jumping, ready for more.

Now we are going to get in a line and run as fast as we can for 50 meters.

Nobody asked why. They just did it because they wanted to.

100-pound Rhodesian ridgeback earns her keep with loyalty

May 5, 1998

I'm standing in line at the veterinarian's office trying to mind my own business, which isn't easy because the place is filled with talking, snarling things.

Ruff-ruff, bow-wow, meow, quack, oink—and those were the people. Meanwhile, a roomful of animals is making slightly less noise with me thinking, what if someone, some mad, impetuous fool were to let his 100-pound Rhodesian ridgeback dog loose in the middle of all this?

Would she unleash Africa on the oinky little pig first or the long-necked goose held around the body and neck by a tiny girl in a pink dress. Or that massively fat tomcat . . ?

"What on earth happened to your dog's back?"

This was from the woman standing just behind me at the receptionist's counter. She's clutching a Louis Vuiton knockoff pet carrier bag like the kind you see people carrying into first class with some yappy little dog inside ready to flysy-whysy with mumsy-wumsy while you fly coach with swine.

"That's disgusting. Did it have surgery?" asked the woman who had Bozo hair, which happens to be a registered trademark of the Bozo Corp., and a mouth on her.

And frankly I'm in no mood because I've already been to work, driven one kid to ballet class and another to karate and now I'm here without a doggie HMO, expecting God only knows what kind of bill because my wife, seeing her 100-pound beast rubbing its butt on a Persian carpet, suspects that it has worms.

"Is that why you're here, because of that thing on your dog's back?" the woman asks, cracking me.

"The thing on her back costs extra," I said. "She's a Rhodesian ridgeback." I run my hand along the Mohawk growing down the beast's spine, growing backward in a direction opposite to the rest of her short, reddish fur. "Get it: ridge-back?"

She wrinkles her nose, joking, "Looks like a mutt."

I have never been what you call a dog person. In fact, this particular dog was a gift to my daughter from a ridgeback-loving friend. Until the death of my favorite idiot, sheep-like dog Clifford, this was our backup dog.

Clifford, despite the fact that everyone figured him to be some kind of purebred, was in fact a pound mutt and the best 20 bucks I ever spent. The ridgeback, Cymbre, cost $600. And whatever she is not, she most definitely is not a mutt.

I point the women toward a dog-breed wall chart. "See, ridgebacks, right there, natural-born killer out of Africa if you happen to be a lion. She's the more or less accidental product of a native ridged dog, European hounds and whatever they mated with in the bush. And the one characteristic they have that you could respect is that they will die for you."

I wasn't kidding. There was a time when Cymbre and I weren't hitting it off. She's aloof, more catlike and elegant than dog-like and slobbering.

Then one day I get followed home by five guys in a car. They drove through a stop sign, nearly hitting me. I honked. They were deeply offended, following close, making obscene gestures while I sit in a car wondering now what?

Pulling into the driveway, one of the kids opens the door, and out comes the tightly strung Cymbre, clued-in by ESP or something: 100 pounds of growling, drooling Afrika hound with heavily muscled rear quarters raised and her long teeth exposed like a postman's acid dream. The five guys look at her, they look at each other, they leave.

Only it takes me 10 minutes to get the dog out of that position. Meanwhile, my view of her changes because I see that she isn't going to move, isn't going to give up or give in this side of death. She now has her own bed by the back door and my affection for life, which isn't so long when you figure that she's 49 in dog years, my age exactly, only she doesn't remember the white album.

Then we see the vet who checks her for the worms she doesn't have. "Sometimes," he said, "dogs just like to scratch their butts."

One itchy butt, $40. Then I spring for the flea repellent drops and promise that I'll work 10 pounds off her. Final bill, including dietary advice ("Feed her less"), $85, and worth it.

He lived with fear of killer

October 29, 1998

It's been five years since votive candles guttered among the heat-wilted flowers laid out where Martin Ganz died during a nothing traffic stop for no reason anybody will ever understand.

Five years of grinding toward a Tuesday morning in Torrance Superior Court, where I went to see the man who used, again for no reason, his .380 pistol on a 55-year-old nurse who happened to be standing outside the Portland supermarket he just strong-armed.

Turns out, prosecutors say, it was the same pistol that killed a young Manhattan Beach cop two days after Christmas in 1993 with the officer's 12-year-old nephew looking on. The nephew was in court Tuesday facing a rotten excuse for a human being named Roger Hoan Brady, a guy who got life without parole for the nurse and could get death here in Torrance.

Either way, this trigger-nuts nebbish is off the street, finally hearing anguished testimony from the now 17-year-old Don Ganz, from the terrified boy locked inside a growing body.

"Brady not what you expected?" asked Larry Altman, the Breeze cop reporter who has been covering this loser from the beginning, traveling to Oregon for his first murder conviction. He points out a half-dozen people in the tiny courtroom whose lives were ruined by the Christmas-week killing.

No, a paunchy sallow-skinned geek isn't what I expected. Of course, neither did I expect a cop-killing in Manhattan Beach. Two shots like heavy stones dropped into water, the impact fanning out, covering family, cops, community, hurting still as young Don Ganz takes the stand, eyes on Roger Hoan Brady, who does not return the gaze.

This was Don Ganz's favorite uncle, remember, the man who asked him on the ride-along, taking him to dinner and out at sunset on the pier, where he asked a stranger to take their picture together, the one hanging on the courtroom exhibit board.

The last life-photo of Martin Ganz, his arm around a happy little boy who would never be quite as happy again, returning to California this week to face the impassive Roger Hoan Brady and to recall a mundane evening of tickets with his uncle showing him the car's emergency call button in a city where no cop had ever been killed. Then the final stop, like all the others only colored now with profound meaning.

Every step, every word, a boy and his uncle two days after Christmas and a silver car in the intersection at 11 p.m. stopped, the pull-over, the drive into the Manhattan Village mall, ordinary.

In the stop-motion view of events he tells the boy, "I'll be right back," approaches the silver car, flashlight up, hand on belt, a man in a car alone, death—if you care to see it that way—reaching for something on the passenger seat.

"I heard a pop. . . . I didn't know what it was. . . . My uncle leaned back like something hit him."

The young man's eyes drill into the emotionless Roger Hoan Brady, tears coming again, the memory of hiding under the dashboard, then looking out to see a man standing in front of the patrol car, muzzle flash, two-handed grip, firing at something on the ground.

Then a gasp and silence. Figuring the shooter gone, he looks out. Only he's still there in that dumb combat stance. Looking toward the car he brings the gun up, aiming at the child who ducks again, facing the passenger door, waiting for the man to come "grab him out."

The term he uses seems to come from the pit of his stomach, "I was deathly afraid." Only the man didn't come for Don Ganz, who would soon press the red button like he was told, leaving on police tape a little boy's terrified cry for help, terror haunting him down the years that this monster would come for him like he came for the favorite uncle he found dying on the ground.

Ironically, it was Don Ganz who came to face the nightmare of Roger Hoan Brady with an eternity between them, an eternity of fear separating an accused murderer from that December night's second victim, the child he didn't kill—not outright.

Repairing broken window brings bonding time for father and son

November 17, 1998

Here's the problem with life, or one of the many problems with life.

OK, it's a nothing problem in a world of pain. Still, a broken window can only be replaced either by someone who has already replaced a broken window or by someone who thinks that they can replace a broken window after reading a how-to book in the hardware store checkout line.

That's me, the guy in line reading the broken-window section of a home repair book that he does not intend to buy, but which he plans to justify by purchasing a 15-by-20-inch piece of glass, glazing compound, a putty knife, a package of licorice whips and these metal pushpin thingies that hold glass in place.

I learned about the pushpins from the book and all about the art of forcing someone to buy licorice whips from the 5-year-old boy who loves two things about the hardware store: licorice whips and sitting on the riding-mowers.

He also likes looking at the aisle nobody is ever on, the one containing uncut chain and huge brass foundation bolts. Used to the kind of namby-pamby projects I take on, he is bowled over by the latent power of mammoth objects.

Beyond that, he comes along because he must come along, driven by whatever it is that makes watching the physical labors of others absolutely irresistible to little boys, old men and dogs.

Luckily, there were no old men on hand if you didn't count me. But there was a small boy and two dogs were lying with black noses pointed in my direction while I prepared to smash out a piece of window glass in our French doors.

"So what do you suppose they call French doors in France?" I asked the boy.

"Doors," he replied as I whacked out the remainder of the glass that had not been whacked out during a fun-time fight between 12-year-old sister and a Rhodesian Ridgeback with the throw-weight of a Russian ICBM.

The rest, if I was to believe the handyman book, would be easy. Or at least it looked easy for the beautifully groomed male model in safety goggles who cleanly tapped away the old glazing compound with a chisel and installed new glass in less than half a page. This while other male models on other pages replaced entire roofs and installed decks big enough to land an F-18.

Obviously the male model performing the glass replacement wasn't dealing with 50-year-old glazing compound that had been hardened to the consistency of spent uranium by 1,100 coats of hearty lead-based paint.

If I had been writing a do-it-your-own-self book based on my experience, replacing this one piece of glass would easily have covered six pages of hammering, gouging and sanding with extra tips on how to clean a cut finger, remove blood from wood and get a kid in and out of a hardware store a second time (because the guy cut the glass wrong) without buying more licorice whips.

I'd also have to include a page or two on the ineffable stuff that comes with child-assisted window repair. Things like actually having the time to talk to a child, which is the learned part of this particular experience. This kid knows, as I knew and my father and grandfather knew, that a male engaged in physical labor is a male who isn't distracted by anything but his own incompetence.

Simply put, the old guy has time to listen. And learn. And what I learned was this, kindergarten isn't easy. In fact, the boy was worried about what he called the "hard numbers" he would be doing in class on Monday. These, it turned out, were the numbers four and five. So on the brown butchers paper the glass came in we wrote fours and fives and talked about important things like Power Rangers and the little girl in class who likes to touch his hair and how he doesn't like little girls especially and especially does not like little girls touching his hair.

Most of all I learned, or relearned, that he's the kind of little kid who shares licorice whips and invests himself heart and soul in a two-hour job that a pro could have accomplished in 10 minutes, only without the warmth.

Years in the wilderness end with an oak table

January 10, 1999

A table should not be made of plastic or particle board, especially particle board. Nor should a good work table be made of plywood or have a crack down the middle for adding dining space. That's because a work table shouldn't be a dining table or one of those sweatshop, computer cubicles people set up at home to remind them of work.

A table should be made of solid wood. Not veneer but seamless wooden planks. Forget the pine-board-country look because this isn't about a look, it's about serious work. Or, in my case, not-so-serious work, which—either way—requires dark wood.

Not light wood stained dark, mind you, but real wood like oak, preferably oak, oak above all other forest products because it speaks of libraries and because it makes us feel far more important than we actually are.

Years ago, more like years and years ago, I had temporary possession of an oak table. I wrote my first newspaper stories on that oak table in what had once been a slave shack bounded by two dirt roads in a North Florida university town.

The house was a rented two-room, shotgun arrangement that must have been built around this massive old creation that easily bore on his broad surface without a jiggle the blue Smith-Corona portable typewriter my sister Josephine bought me for high school graduation.

The scene was probably nowhere near as idyllic as I recall, but what I do recall is that wonderful table and a huge double-hung window facing out on Spanish moss and dust from those roads. That and a big blue-eyed, black cat named Pushkin, a rat serial killer who would sleep away those long Southern afternoons on the typed pages that covered that glorious flat surface.

I even made arrangements to buy the table when I moved out for some months of traveling only to find, upon my return, that the table had been sold along with the cabin to a pair of artsy guys who decorated the place half to death.

What followed was years in the plastic wilderness, decades punctuated with false table tops and inadequate work surfaces facing windows that faced nothing at all, with only one improvement over that slave shack work space, a computer.

Computers are, of course, a hack's dream. Only the other part of that dream was missing all this time and only partially realized in a large plastic-like table that more or less looked out on our back yard. Unlike the window of memory, this view never ceased reminding me that everything growing out there required work.

But I had to wonder, did Hemingway gaze out across Paris from his clean, well-lighted place and think about replacing a few broken roof tiles?

OK, so you've read Hemingway and I'm not him. Still, the point applies, if you want to let the muses run amok you got to at least supply them with a changing room and some clean towels.

That's what I was thinking, changing rooms and clean towels, when I lost my work space to a 12-year-old who also kept the plastic desk because it could hold both books and the aquarium containing Fang, her gopher snake.

Still, I did have room for a table in our under-used living room. So why not scrounge up a table, a real table. Only furniture stores don't sell real tables. They sell things that look like real tables but aren't. They sell tables that are new and made to look old or new and look like they belong in the dining room of some guy who wears white shoes and a cardboard belt.

That's when I turned to antique stores, to many antique stores, to tables that were almost what I wanted. But I didn't want almost this time, I wanted perfect. Or perfect for me, which I found, finally, in the last place I looked. A huge oak library table, an 1890s, solid oak monster that would require four men, a small boy and me to get it in the front door.

It's a wonderful piece of work, too, a fat- legged, map-drawered, Ohio-made creation that looks ridiculously expensive and wasn't. Now it sits before a huge window facing my lethal avocado tree, facing me, looking up at me, I swear, lending its fragrant, peaceful, DNA-saturated self smoothly to the palms of my hands while pleasing my heart, I swear, like little else.

Or little else that isn't alive, 5-years-old and presently using the under-table space as a tent, adding himself to its history, to whatever it is that matchless old stuff like this conveys to us right now and to whoever is lucky enough to own it next.

6 girls under 1 roof equals prom madness

April 25, 1999

Over lunch in Hermosa Beach I was telling a friend about the activities that consumed our house the previous Saturday, which was prom night, an evening traditionally fraught with arcane customs and practices that would baffle an ordinary man.

An ordinary man, in this case, being a man who did not grow up with sisters—as I did—a man who has not fathered two daughters and is not married to a stylish woman and just doesn't understand that there really is no understanding this sort of thing, not for men, ever.

But I did know what to expect when I was told that six girls were preparing for the junior prom in our house.

Of course, it would have been nice if I had been told before 5 p.m. when they were already preparing and I was just back from my horrific afternoon run and informed that all three of our bathrooms were occupied.

Too bad a man can't really be prepared for the frantic activity that began weeks before with dress locating. Here's how it works: The girls in this particular set buy a new dress for their school prom and borrow a dress for lesser proms at other schools.

This was a lesser prom, so they borrowed. Unfortunately, close friendship does not guarantee a body-type match. That is why I was seeing girls that I barely knew in those two weeks, girls of approximately my daughter's height and weight bearing long fabric creations in clear plastic bags.

As I understood it, my Caitlin loaned her blue gown to Alisha, who had loaned her red gown to Amy, who loaned her black gown to some other Caitlin, who didn't especially like it, traded the black gown to Kelly, who liked it more than the pink gown she borrowed from Kelly II (I think), who was going to wear a sequined number borrowed from Diedra. Or was it Amanda? Anyway, I pretty much lost it after that.

However, if you have ever purchased a prom dress, you know how grateful a parent can be for all the borrowing. Trouble is, when getting-dressed-time finally arrived, two of the girls didn't really like the dresses they had borrowed and one had gotten deodorant on hers and, well, they heard that Mrs. Bogert had some nice gowns.

Which is true. Mrs. Bogert does, only they didn't actually hear this. What they did was spot the gowns she had taken out for our own daughter and they just seemed nicer than what they had borrowed.

Besides, all three of the girls in question hover just below 6 feet tall while my wife is 5-foot-9. Isn't this a wonderful coincidence. That's how three of my wife's gowns, four pairs of her shoes and many pieces of her jewelry left the house that evening.

But not before they got ready, a process that required three hours, three showers in three separate bathrooms, all the hot water in four counties, 18 towels, six curling irons and six hair dryers—the use of which blacked out cities as far away as Cleveland while creating an unholy scream surpassing the decibel level of the entire Torrance air show.

There was also great tension, something most men

and boys might not understand. That's because men preparing en masse for such an outing usually engage in loud talk, towel-snapping, butt-grabbing and what would definitely be fighting-word insults if everyone involved weren't such good friends.

Girls, on the other hand, are intense. That's because hair is involved, which naturally involves our daughter who happens to be the girl (there's always one) who is good at hair, six heads of it in wildly different styles.

This while crisis after crisis was encountered and overcome. Tights emerged from wrappers ripped, shoes suddenly did not match dresses (maybe it's just the light), makeup was not quite right (again, the light), somebody forgot her lip liner while every one of these svelte creatures asked if their backsides looked too big. They eventually emerged from total chaos and bathroom steam in clouds of perfume, six radiant young women, gowned and gloved like something out of a 19th century novel, walking straight into the camera-zap of parents who weren't going to miss this even if their girls were getting ready somewhere else.

Then they were gone to boys. Bye, see ya. Just like that, the lovely creatures vanished into night.

So I told all this to my friend over lunch because it was funny and because of all it said about life's passage and about the latent promise and mystery of youth.

Then, back in the newsroom, the first video was coming in from a massacre in a place called Littleton, and it suddenly seemed like so much more.

Boy finds out umbrellas can fly—and angels might, too

June 29, 1999

We have this nutty idea that bad things happen to children only when we're not there or because we are not there. The cosmic error here being that if we are there, then they are safe.

And I was right THERE Sunday at the beach, dad and a 5-year-old boy in a manatee-decorated swimsuit, dad slathering scrawny kid shoulders with No. 9000 sunblock, dad who would never dream of letting the child go near the water alone because he is a worrying control freak.

Just then, just after noon on an almost windless day straight out of heaven, the big beach umbrella we were sitting under gets wind-lifted out of the sand. Down it goes in an instant, or maybe a quarter-instant, the sharp aluminum point up-thrusting. . . . Did I mention that I was maybe 3 feet away from him when the umbrella point struck him in the eye?

The boy has beautiful eyes. His sisters say they are too beautiful for a boy. They are certainly too pretty to be defiled by a flying wedge of aluminum. He had blood on his hand where it covered his eye, blood I could see in the flat-second it took for him to get hit and for me to be there prying the hand loose.

I once had to retrieve his sister from an emergency room after a car crash. Nothing wrong, they told me over the phone, she's fine. Only when I got there she was still strapped down to a backboard and nobody had actually examined her closely enough to say that she was, in fact, just fine.

That same run-through feeling was on me as I pulled his hand away. He was shaking. I was shaking, not in the hands but everywhere else, and there was almost no damage at all. But listen: The sharp metal umbrella point cut a clean one-eighth-inch swath through his eyelashes. Which meant that it had missing the eye by less than an eyelash-width.

There was a small cut on his eyelid too. That's where the blood was coming from, a cut that didn't even need a bandage. Trouble is, they don't make a bandage that can make a parent avoid considering what might have happened on a sunny day when he was right there beside me and things were perfect.

Which led the boy and I, as we sat philosophically sipping Cokes in the post-accident haze, to consider close calls and angels. Actually, he brought up the angel business, saying: "It was probably an angel that saved me just now. Which struck me as odd because I don't remember ever talking to him about angels, and I know darn well that his Scottish Presbyterian mother never did.

So I told him my angel story because it is diverting and because we weren't doing much else except looking at the sea through four healthy eyes. I told him about how I was given, when I was about his age, what the Catholics call a holy card. On it was printed a picture of a little boy walking through a scary forest accompanied by this huge angel. White-robed and massively winged, she hovered over the oblivious little boy, shielding him against, I don't know, wolves, lions, evil men in trench coats.

In a life sodden with religious artifacts, this printed flight-of-fancy is the only one that took because I recognized her instantly as the angel who had saved me from a near-fatal bout with Asian flu in 1958 and from bicycle and sled accidents that should have killed me outright. A dozen near-misses and she was there like a supernatural helicopter gunship.

The kicker, I explained to the fast-recovering boy, was how I once was talking to a psychic in Palos Verdes, a wonderful woman who asked me if I knew that a large and hugely winged angel was standing behind me?

The kid asked, "What's a psychic?" So I explained that a psychic—if you believe in that sort of thing, and who knows the limit of what a 5-year-old can believe—is someone who can sense things that others can't. Adding, "And she saw your angel?"

"She said that she did," I explained, not mentioning how the psychic's words had made me shiver because it was as if she had looked straight through me into something that I can't even pretend to understand.

"Think she's still watching you?"

"The psychic?"

"The angel. Do you think the angel is still watching?"

"Don't know."

"Well, I think she just started watching me."

I think she is, too.

A eulogy for wise guys and the sacred Italian bond

July 8, 1999

Nums, Tony Fats, Little Nicky and Eddie Bobo all deferred to Big Bobby the Cook and his wife, Angela, who was dark and pretty in a voluptuous, critical-mass Italian way.

I wasn't surprised back in 1973, between college and Europe, that the entire staff was Italian, every last one of them down from New York and Jersey to work in the kitchen of a Florida seafood restaurant owned by a tiny Italian named Little Tony—he of the big Fedora hats and tall girlfriends, he who so beautifully acted out the oily good life with the monster Lincoln and few words.

Everybody played the Italian greeting game wit. Little Tony, with the fawning body language and the tutto tutto rispetto. Angela, on the other hand, could complain about everything, about the waiters, about the heat, about the French Canadian tourists who'd ask her to take pictures of them in their lobster bibs before stiffing her.

Angela had certain rights as Little Tony's niece and Big Bobby's wife and the mother of three young men who did not accompany them down to Florida when Bobby got out of the joint on work-release.

In truth, everybody working in the kitchen that summer, when I was still young and not so quickly clued, was out on work-release and . . . well, it finally clicked. In fact, it should have clicked the day Big Bobby hired me, first refusing my application for a salad chef job, then hiring me after asking, "You Italian?"

Sensing a point of entry, I said, "My mother's from Foggia."

Guess what, his father was from Foggia. So already we had this sacred bond. We were both raised by maniacs who sent us to Catholic schools, to hard-eyed nuns, to church every morning. Only I went to college and Big Bobby became a barber, a barber with a two-chair shop, a barber with sons in private school, three Cadillacs, a $500,000 house, a vacation condo in Miami and it was only a matter of time before the IRS saw that Big Bobby was making book in the back room.

Big Bobby took good care of the people in his kitchen. We ate well, worked hard, and I have to admit that I liked these slick guys with their cigars and racing forms, their Scotch, their trips to Atlantic City and their jail talk.

Nums, the chief salad guy, wore this huge gold cross around his neck and called his mother every day from the kitchen phone. Like everywhere, calling long distance on the company line was forbidden. Except, in this case, when you needed to call your mother.

Num—being the first three letters of a last name that I wouldn't use on a bet—had just finished six years for manslaughter. "The one I didn't do, they whack me for," he explained. Nums taught me how to make 20-gallon vats of Thousand Island dressing. That's how I found out that he had been in prison.

"Where'd you learn how to do this?" I asked.

All casual, "In the pen."

Really, they were the best, do-anything-for-you people. They'd come by and start your car if your battery was dead or loan you money no-questions-asked if you were short a few fazools. They'd always ask me if I called my mother, if I kept in touch with my uncles. If I said no they'd say, "Oh, you gotta call your uncles." Why? "Because they're your uncles."

Trouble was, they all had this other side, the side that revealed itself the night a bunch of drunks out of a dentists convention insulted Angela out front where she was playing hostess. I've seen some bad stuff. But the violence in these men was breathtaking.

They just piled out and started punching. No words. No threats. No posturing. The warmest guys in the world one minute and all the violence in the world the next, which I bring up only because Mario Puzo dying last week reminded me of them and how their favorite movie—the one they talked about all the time and made comparisons to all the time—was naturally "The Godfather."

They loved the whole leave-the-gun-bring-the-cannoli thing, the whole never-betray-the-family, loyalty-and-silence thing because it made them feel far more noble than they actually were.

It made their failed hood lives seem special, like something out of a samurai film, like something out of Italy and, more importantly, like something out of America too. Mario Puzo's work did that for guys like that and for guys who weren't quite like that, but who understood anyway. And for that he deserves our respect—tutto tutto rispetto.

Generations come together in cul-de-sac

August 6, 1999

We'd meet in front of my house, Everett Hughes and me. Mr. Hughes, I always called him. Out there ahead of the tall hedges where not much goes on he joked, one day, about my son being 90 years his junior. In his house up at the end of the cul-de-sac he had a sword that belonged to his uncle, a Civil War veteran.

It was wonderful human connection between the ages, a little boy and a 95-year-old man, both alive out where our street empties into the real world.

Along here he'd come with his wife, Ruth, every night and morning. Late night and early morning so I'd see them when I was up feeding a new baby. In cold and rain they'd walk arm and arm in the old style. Ruth was once a college drama teacher washed out of her job when they had their first child many, not-terribly-woman-friendly decades ago.

When that first child died a few years ago, Mr. Hughes stopped to tell me what he learned. Looking off into the distance he made a point that binds us: "She was my baby."

A petroleum engineer, he once helped devise the formula that kept gasoline from glopping up carburetors.

And all along he did it right, never letting up on life, never giving in. He played badminton for years, athletic even in extreme old age, walking with Ruth who would die six years ahead of him.

A university medical researcher in retirement, he had a way with few words. At a memorial service for his wife he mentioned the now-absent hand he held for so many years, the hand he pursued fervently on a college campus when they were young. Now he would go to sleep without her. He said this at a memorial service in their backyard under avocado trees.

Assembled were people they knew from the book and bicycle club, from hiking, from staying active in a real neighborhood, a vital link whether we recognize it or not. That's because it's not right, this now-common separation of ages, this going off to hot places to live an old life, this putting the young in one city and the old in another because little boys—and I know this to be true—need to look up and see a man 90 years their senior. As I still needed to speak to a man of my father's generation.

I don't know exactly how that happens, how we rise and fall and somehow lose ourselves in life. Old here, young there, contemporaries almost nowhere as years pass, elders scatter and die. Then one day I'm standing out by the hedges when he walks past. I tell him that we have a son on the way, some state of affairs for a 45-year-old.

And into all this he smiles, telling me that I am a young man, saying: "I think I was getting ready to retire when my last boy went off to college." Which was exactly my position, or future position, if I came out as lucky as he did, riding his old bike, wearing a big old white engineer's helmet, driving a car well past 90, smiling, smart and wise past 90.

Several years ago he gave me his autobiography, an illustrated and beautifully written life story he compiled for his five children and their children. Pictures in it of weddings, of babies long grown and times lived that you can't read about in history books because they don't cover the minor and miraculous brush strokes of life.

It stayed with me how he wrote of playing with that Civil War sword on a Midwest farm, how he remembered the early days of petroleum engineering and how his family figured so importantly into all his long life, all of them well educated and doing well.

In the months after the memorial service under the avocado trees, he'd walk by same as always. The same at first, then gradually slower. Things finally catching up, saddling him, talking away his fine senses. Still, of his wife's death he once said: "It's just the life cycle coming around." As he spoke he traced that circle in the air with his parchment-skin hand, adding, "I'm learning how to cook."

Then came the caretakers, the women who watched him when he refused to leave the house he came to 35 years ago in good retirement. No Florida, no Arizona. A regular neighborhood where people live, there to be part of it all, a fixture in the life of a little boy who could look up and see a man 95 years old and still going, towering way up there, ancient like men I saw as a child, men with eyes no longer completely of this world.

That's how he went at the end. Walking slowly and alone, he told me one afternoon in early spring, "My voice is going."

Then he went completely into that other world, into a place where there had better be points for a life beautifully lived.

A clear choice for Uncle Henry: live forever or die trying

June 11, 2000

Last year my 5-year-old L.A. boy told me, "I like being at Florida because Uncle Henry is at Florida and because alligators are at Florida."

We named the kid Ian Henry after adopted uncle Welcom Henry Watson Jr., who was himself named after his dad, Welcom Sr., a lawyer and man of foresight who settled in Fort Lauderdale, Fla., back when the town was all youthful possibility.

I certainly never imagined such a life connection back in 1967 when I first spotted Henry in our high school pool spitting water and wearing his trademark smirk. I was 18, he was 15 and had already told Reesa Hairston that he was going to marry her.

He announced this, she told me over the phone the other day, when they were 13. Years later, after he finished Harvard and started law school, after Reesa did everything to shake the guy, they were finally married.

Much, much later, after 26 years and three wonderful

daughters, he'd call this long infatuation "commitment without reason." This is the same person who would show up all casual in Reesa's college classes a thousand miles from Harvard, causing one of her exasperated boyfriends to ask me, "Who is this Henry Watson?"

When it came to his intended, Henry was a stalker. Only in Henry this was charming. In fact, everything about Henry was charming in a monstrously intelligent, slightly off-center way that allowed him to chase a girl until she said yes.

When Reesa called to tell me that she was getting married, I asked, "To who?"

To Henry, the man who would give up lawyering after 17 years, saying that he had "become the kind of slovenly attorney" that he couldn't stand. So he started a software company called Real Estate Expert Systems Associates or REESA—just in case you thought that this man didn't love absolutely.

Somewhere in there he also became my brother. A year ago this month, he became a brother with colon cancer. Only this was Henry with cancer, Henry being the guy who would walk my children down the street when we absolutely had to be somewhere else to show them the black iguana living in a neighbor's mango tree. Or he'd road-trip us to Key Largo for lunch at some gun-runner diner.

He was also a fantastic sailor, having learned his craft as a boy, alone in small boats, a boy who would grow into a man who knew more about the things of this Earth than anybody I know. And that included cancer. On re-read, all that Henry e-mailed on the subject started with this line, "By Thursday night (days after diagnosis) I had the clinical side down and this phrase in my head, `I'm going to live forever or die trying.' I've also opted to bypass the denial phase and get on with it."

After surgery revealed a run-rampant tumor, Reesa

e-mailed: "Henry is not morbid and even in the worst hours still has that stupid sense of humor."

Henry e-mailed on July 9: "I've decided to live."

He decided that Henry Watson wasn't a statistic. So he did everything, chemotherapy, vitamins, exercise and health foods while becoming an even more thoughtful Henry. When JFK Jr. died, he recalled himself at age 10 in another message: "I remember standing in the back yard and crying for a pretty long time. This time I was grieving not so much for the current loss but for a loss long ago that was never reconciled."

"Today was a good day," he wrote just after Thanksgiving, after many ups and downs. "On Thursday I thought of all the things for which I am thankful."

Henry liked Thanksgiving, I discovered a few years ago on a steaming summer day, when we walked into a combination dry cleaners/antique shop to pick up his laundry and he impulse-bought a turkey-shaped platter.

When we were down last August I drove him to his vitamin infusion therapy. Sitting side by side on lounge chairs, we talked about how we fool ourselves into thinking that we actually have a stated life span coming when all we ever really have is the moment.

The next night, after our last family meal together, I told him that he owed me dinner. "I get it," he said with a smirk. "I have to repay you next trip."

Only there was no next trip, just e-mail and one last phone call to the clinic in Tijuana where he died on June 2 with his parents and Reesa at his side. He was 48.

Another friend, trying to cheer me up during this last dark week, told me to picture Henry's version of heaven. And I did, recalling a bright October day 10 years ago. We're off Miami heeling hard-over in his sailboat with the rails plowing warm blue/green water and Henry at the wheel grinning, hooked into a place that is neither sky or sea but somewhere glorious, eternal and in between.

Aunt Mary was last connection to a wild and wonderful past

August 6, 2000

As far back as I can remember, my Aunt Mary had this wonderful head of wildly curly white hair. She looked to me like George Washington on the dollar bill, only shorter and a lot more fun.

Mary was the eldest of four daughters born in Italy to dirt farmers—my grandparents—who beat it to America the minute they got World War I out of the way. Which was just as well. Back then, Italy was a great place to suffer through a short life. Mary once told me how, as a little girl, one of her baby brothers died in her arms.

Mother and father, Carmella and Giovanni, were out tilling dry earth and she was looking after a sick baby whose name she could not even recall. Luckily Carmella had 12 children, cut down to four ornery survivors by the time they got to Ellis Island and factory jobs in upstate New York.

There's nothing unusual in this immigrant saga, not in the the way it happened or in how it's being so quickly forgotten as the old Italians pass on, leaving us with fables incomprehensible to American descendants who think a nice place to live is a birthright.

Close as I was to the experience, it was second hand

to me, a collection of stories so hard-scrabbled they'd sound like fiction if so many families didn't tell the same tale. If you need more verification, visit the museum at Ellis Island.

These were tough times. Yanking kids from school at 12 wasn't unusual, which is what Carmella and Giovanni did to their girls. Then again, maybe that was more an Italian thing to do because many Jewish families in the same position pooled money to send the best kid off to college.

That's why Mary and sisters Rose (my mother), Polly and Mickey (American names given them by American teachers who found the girls nicely outgoing) ended up living by their natural intelligence and gab.

Mary did all sorts of things, like being married to my uncle Nick for about 3,000 years and never falling out of love with him. Aside from that, and being Nick Jr.'s mother, she sold cosmetics door to door. Later, when three of the four sisters moved their entire families to Florida, she got a job waitressing at a famous deli near the beach.

You know those fake wise-cracking, call-you-honey waitresses you meet at fake diners. My Aunt Mary was really like that. She remembered names and orders. She spoke Italian for fun and became pals with Rocky Marciano, one of her regulars. The former heavyweight champion of the world and my aunt, buddies.

She served Mantle and Maris down for the Yankees' spring training. Best of all, we'd go in after school and, no matter what we ordered, she'd write us up for a soda—80 cents. So it was a bad moral example, but she had a way with kids.

I should know because Mary was also my co-mother, raising my cousin and me together in a time and place where kids like us didn't question blood authority. It was an unspoken contract dreamed up in some ancient time when children were wholly accepted and deeply loved. This was the natural order, crying to Aunt Mary and listening to Aunt Mary, who was a witch in any case.

I mean that in the best possible sense because Mary came uneducated out of a peasant culture that found its cures in the soil and in a brand of Christianity that came ready-mixed with dark paganism. The evil eye was in our lives and Mary knew the holy words to cast it off. She learned the holy secrets as all women learned them, from other women. From her all cures flowed. She could drive off headaches and stomach flu, colds and fever by praying foreign words, barely audible, in what I took to be the language of God. Then she'd lay a quarter on you for a candy.

Mary could interpret dreams, too. Later, I'd hear of people doing that—psychiatrists, Freudians. I had Mary reassuring me that a dream of death wasn't a bad dream, just a message from people who loved you, people in heaven, people you'd get to be with someday if you were good and they had anything to say about it.

This is the same woman who let Nick and me get away with murder, the only aunt in the bunch who would take us to the beach, who would treat us to movies and let us sleep out on the porch. She was my mother's opposite, a blessing.

I was talking about all this the other day with cousin Nick, who had just made Mary's funeral arrangements.

"The stuff we got away with, I'm surprised she didn't bury us," he said, as we recalled illegal firecracker spectaculars and him driving us around in his mother's 1951 Dodge, the one she called Queenie, when he was 12 and unlicensed.

Mary died last week, the last sister, the end catching her at 91 in an imaginary world that wasn't treating her too badly.

"She'd tell me about her days," Nick said, "about shopping and lunch, about taking a walk with Aunt Rose. All this she did without ever leaving the nursing home."

Wonderful cook and magical gardener, a reader of heavenly signs, Mary was circulation-shot and mind-gone at the very end. She was also the last of the old Italians, my final connection to a vanished life that leaned heavily on family and believed absolutely in love.

Nick is going to spread her ashes over the ocean like she asked.

In delivering a college freshman, be ready to take some heat

August 31, 2000

Let's get the sad part over with up front, sadness being an inevitable component of sending a kid packing. After all, we raise our children right, educating and nurturing them like prize puppies while doing our very best not to be horrible and embarrassing like our own parents—only to wind up being horrible and embarrassing anyway.

Still, we managed to put together our first college freshman package. She dances, plays piano, draws. She's a 17-year-old who would be at home in 14th-century Florence. Then, after all that parental slave labor, we dropped her off at college, in a dorm room like something out of Fort Dix and drove away—see ya.

There is no way around the sense of loss and the feeling that this may not be the very best way to go, while firmly believing that this is absolutely the best way to go. After all, this is what our parents did to us after they, at our age, got dropped off at World War II.

So what's to complain about? Life is difficult at best and never more difficult than the day one realizes that one must rent an SUV to carry all the garbage the kid needs for college. That's how we ended up with a gas-slurping Dodge Durango, a battering ram that our departing daughter thought was too small, but actually wasn't, after the rest of us limited our packing to one toothbrush each.

This, by the way, is the same daughter who put a few things off until the very last day. Nothing important, just immunizations, buying a computer (really, nothing easier than finding the right computer), buying a microwave oven and buying everything that she needed to turn a Tucson dorm room into home.

"I'm sooooo busy," she said as she pursued the real work of summer, which included a job as a hostess and saying goodbye to about 1,000 friends. That and watching the entire "Godfather" saga at my urging because all children should know why Moe Green gets it in the eye.

Shut up. These are important questions.

So are ones like, "Did you pack vitamins, Tylenol, cold capsules, your insurance card, a dictionary, tissues, towels, soap, bleach, Lysol spray?" Now that I think about it, why do parents act like college dormitories are as germ-infested as 14th Century Paris?

I need to mention here that temperatures in Tucson during the summer are approximately the same as those at the sun's core. I mention this because it was a tad hot as all five of us relieved the Dodge of its rear-view-obliterating cargo and moved it into a closet-size room near the very top of a very tall building.

This might not have been such a difficult task, mind you, had 2,000 other heat-and-child-defeated parents not been attempting the same thing at the exact same moment in late, late August. Plus, this is a university with a university's unhinged sense of order, which is to say that one doesn't go directly to one's room without first obtaining a pink slip from Room A, to be delivered to Room B, where freshmen are issued proper forms so that a key can be obtained in Room C, which is conveniently located in a dark cellar.

On the positive side, this gave us plenty of time to move microwave, linens, shelves, under-bed drawers, posters, books, photographs of 1,000 friends, VCR (formerly MY VCR) and more shoes than Imelda Marcos has into one vast pile on a sizzling sidewalk while a guy with a Russian accent screamed, “No park here. No park!”

Well, let me tell you something, pal. The big-fella Dodge parks wherever the heck it likes. And it did as we moved from standing around with a vast pile of junk to standing in line waiting for an elevator with a vast pile of junk with all the other moms and dads who seemed to be asking the same shrill question, “Did you bring the Lysol?”

Meanwhile, the incoming freshman endured this final blast of baby-talk-concern with looks that screamed, “Stop torturing me and just go away, puleeze!”

Only before we could vanish into the cactus desert we had to drive all over town buying $300 worth of minor items that the kid forgot. Then, heat-diseased and mind-wasted, we congregated in her room, where things could have spun seriously out of control had little brother not gotten his dirty little shoes on the new Tommy Hilfiger bedspread.

Nothing like a mundane scullery task while saying goodbye, saying it like we’d see her tomorrow or soon thereafter. But it doesn’t stop me from going into her empty room at bedtime just to say good night.

Walking the Las Vegas Strip with a little fear and loathing

September 8, 2000

This is the end of all travelogues, the last stop, Las Vegas—a place you can say absolutely anything about and still have it be true.

Of course, I knew this going in. Everybody knows this going in. That's why people go. Me, I was there largely because I didn't want to drive all the way from the Grand Canyon to L.A. in one SUV-powered, gas-sucking swoop. So why not see the place I have avoided like anthrax my entire life?

Besides, I have a 13-year-old daughter who somehow knows in her heart that Vegas is her kind of town. This being the same daughter who, as a small child, used to slip adults buck tips saying, "Buy yourself something nice." Which leads me to believe absolutely in reincarnation. In her case, the reincarnation of Carlo Gambino.

"Maybe they'll let me play blackjack," she wondered as we crossed Hoover Dam, where I discovered that kids aren't as impressed by hydroelectric power as they once were.

"Lot of cement," our 6-year-old offered. The other one, Ms. Gambino, added, "Is this low tech or what?"

Then it was on to Vegas, a place that would look no

different than any other desperate strip-mall-choked rising city of the American Desert were it not for The Strip. And you don't even have to go there to know about The Strip.

It's a place that long ago invaded what's left of the world's consciousness as a symbol of all that is decadent, evil and overdone, all that is soulless and utterly without moral character or behavioral breaker switches of any kind—thus making it immensely attractive to everyone.

Literally, everyone. Young people, old people, people from all foreign lands, people from places where you didn't know they even had people. People walking the desert night drinking out of bongs, people with plastic coin cups growing out of their hands, people wearing slot machine credit cards around their necks like Marley's ghost, people actually tethered to slots machines by card and lanyard.

There are people here who will run across six lanes of traffic jam to watch the Bellagio fountain squirt water to canned opera music when it should be squirting, and I feel strongly about this, to the immortal Francis Albert Sinatra out of gratitude and respect.

We didn't have to sprint. In fact, we didn't even have to leave our room at Bally's, selected because our medical writer said the place had good elevators. Which it did. It was also the only hotel there that didn't seem to have some kind of idiot theme.

Pyramids, Arabian nights, Italian over-ripeness, Paris with a huge Eiffel Tower just outside our window so we had that and the Bellagio fountain schmaltzing with "Time To Say Goodbye" every half-hour in the death heat.

Somebody obviously, or much more than obviously, decided that gambling wasn't enough. No, the suckers needed oddly shaped buildings, buildings that remind us of New York or Venice or we ain't going. And never mind that once you are past these grand facades, once you pass into the very heart of the out-of-time beast, you are always in the same exact place.

It might even be the same people for all I know, like in that Jim Carrey movie where everyone is an actor except him. Actually, this was worse than that. Everyone here looked like the same person. There were old folks, the infirm and heavily smoking folks playing the slots, eye-glazed.

Then there are card players and craps people at long tables you wouldn't go near on a bet because who the heck knows how to shoot craps. Besides, there should be a rule that nobody should be able to blow on anybody's dice unless he is wearing an undone tuxedo tie and a big-haired woman.

But seriously ladies and germs, where is the fun? Everybody looked like they were making bank deposits, wearing ATM faces. At best, slightly bemused or downright dopey like the big, jerky drunk boys bumping into people on the sidewalks. Or completely idiotic like me, a man with children walking The Strip looking for nothing and finding it, being slipped handbills by street people—handbills featuring naked women who want to come visit special you. You being a guy who might as well be wearing a bowling shirt, a guy with small children walking a clogged street on a broiling night when he is handed . . . never mind.

That's because the power dam is there to illuminate a black hole in the desert where my wife tries to win an evil-red Jaguar off a computerized slot machine. It would have served her right if she got it.

Cake, ice cream and a healthy dose of Extra Strength Tylenol

November 12, 2000

There were 17 children on the front lawn last Sunday. Seventeen 7-year-olds, one 10-pound bag of Smart & Final popcorn, 4 gallons of apple juice, 10 kilos of Oreo cookies, 5 pounds of potato chips and 2 gallons of ice cream.

Seventeen 7-year-olds and two Extra Strength Tylenol, fours cups of coffee, one large chocolate cake with "Happy Birthday Ian" boldly scrawled on its surface in white icing. Seventeen boys and girls and 35 balloons, one roll of white crepe paper, one cut-out sign reading "Happy Birthday Ian" and I am not even sure how many of the party-goers can read.

But they can all run, jump and scream like howler monkeys in the rented jumping castle, the rented jumping castle that was supposed to show up at noon, but arrived at 7 a.m. in the van of a happy young man who remarked, "Early, huh?"

Oh yes, very early, and we had 17 little boys and girls coming over to take part in fun that had to be organized. Otherwise, my little boy told me, his friends would "go crazy."

Of course, determining if a 7-year-old is crazy or just normally crazed is a matter of perspective. At one point during the long afternoon a friend of ours walked past the front lawn battle-mayhem and asked over the hedge, "How can you take this?"

Easy. Two Extra Strength Tylenol and four cups of coffee and I was fine, hoisting the Barney pinata that we bought because we thought it was a T-Rex. Only it was actually Barney and square beyond belief in the eyes of my boy who, nonetheless, helped his sister stuff it with three bags of candy.

Only the bags weighed 5 pounds each, making Barney one heavy purple dinosaur that had to be raised and lowered on a thin line borrowed from Scott, my neighbor, who also loaned us his football-player son Matthew, whose second birthday party we attended on his front lawn 13 years ago. Which I present as Exhibit A: Time does indeed fly.

His friend, my 14-year-old daughter, also helped—or promised to help as they ate hot dogs and played a OO7 video game, explaining that their promised help did not extend to balloon-inflating or paper-stringing but was limited to the more weighty task of crowd control.

Did I mention that the crowd was a bunch of 7-year-olds, sweet children happily dropped off by parents who happily sped away. One mom didn't even get out. "See you at 4," she told her son who bounded directly into the chaos—chaos being the natural state of small children fueled with juice and junk food.

Meanwhile, the jumping castle burned off kid energy like a refinery flare. But direction was needed so I told jokes, "Guy walked up to me on the street the other day saying he hadn't eaten in a week . . . I told him, 'You should force yourself.' Hey, what is this, an audience or an oil painting?"

A clown would have been worth another hundred bucks.

Then we ran three-legged races, egg-on-spoon races

and freeze-frame contests with the children competing furiously for prizes my wife picked up at Rite Aid. A minor revolt took place when it turned out that everybody wanted the squishy, gel-filled balloons instead of these really neat phosphorescent stars that stick to the bedroom ceiling and glow like a cheap plastic universe all night. And I should know because I had them in my dorm room in college 100 years before the advent of bouncy-castle technology.

So they argued and tried to cheat in every way imaginable, everyone but the girls who played fair, moved steadily and won. This while the boys ran wild, failed to think ahead and generally behaved like wolves.

I took the pictures as seven candles were blown out, as cake was cut, as presents were torn open like ammo cases at Normandy. I fired off a couple of rolls because I have been here before with two other children on this same lawn. Only now I know that I am shooting pictures for future yearbooks and for senior-year photo retrospectives so everybody can look back and laugh at how little they all were, how cute and sweet and how absolutely fleeting it all was.

Getting needled about decorating the traditional agave cactus

November 28, 2000

I should mention the headgear first. One 7-year-old, mine, wore a red batting helmet even though he wasn't at that moment playing baseball. The other, Christian from next door, showed up in a cap featuring at its top a large, fabric catfish.

The choice of head covering goes a long way toward describing the quality of help I had when it came time to string Christmas lights Saturday afternoon, a day when I didn't actually mean to take part in an activity that has come to symbolize male ineptitude. It just turned out that way when I went down to OSH to buy a part for a broken toilet.

OSH didn't, of course, have the part. They never do. But it is a much more pleasant hardware shopping experience than visiting a huge warehouse store. But what is more wasteful than a wasted trip to what my wife—24 years here from Britain—still insists on calling "the ironmongers"?

Luckily, the ironmonger did offer tiny Christmas lights. Actually, they have been offering lights, fake Christmas trees and light-up plastic reindeer since last July so it was no surprise that they had the lights I needed to decorate the two huge agave cactus that grace the street-facing corner of our disheveled property.

This lunatic plan was hatched in 110-degree heat last summer in Tucson, where I saw massive saguaro cactus strung with tiny lights. Having grown up in an unyieldingly hot climate where people wrap coconut palms with holiday lights, I found this desert flora adaptation infinitely appealing.

Only coconut palms don't have needles. Or, in the case of agave cactus, the ability to be distilled into tequila. That and saw-like edges and, at the tip of each flipper-like arm, a needle like a tenpenny nail.

So I had at hand on Saturday two lethal agave, 500 tiny white lights and two little helpers who accompanied me outside full of fine resolution and honorable intent. That and Christmas-like 80-degree heat and a clear determination to turn common, everyday, deadly garden plants into what my 14-year-old daughter would call "the merest suggestion of Christmas decorations."

In retrospect, I probably should have gone for a full-house light display with a plywood Santa leaning suggestively against the chimney. Sure, you could fall off a house and die instantly. But better to die fast than suffer death by 1,000 cactus cuts while two little boys stand nearby carrying on a conversation more surreal than my decorating task.

Boy One: "A long time ago what did people do when they got cut on a cactus?"

Boy Two: "They were lucky because the doctors weren't any good."

Boy One: "How were they lucky if the doctors weren't any good?"

Boy Two: "They'd call Jesus and he'd come over and fix them."

Boy One: "But what happened when Jesus wasn't there anymore?"

Boy Two: "Then the doctors had to start reading books about how to fix cuts."

I did mention that they were wearing these peculiar hats, didn't I? They were also getting bored with serious theological conversation and light-stringing the deadly agave and were wanting to move toward activity involving a small, blue football.

But I couldn't quit. No matter how many times they asked, "How much longer now?" No matter how many pedestrians joked, "You can start on my house when you're finished here," I couldn't give in. Nor could I be deterred by a neighbor who looked up at me where I stood teetering over the vicious plants on a ladder to say: "A friend of mine fell into cactus last year on a hunting trip. He hasn't been the same since."

But who can say with certainty that not being the same isn't an improvement in some people. Especially in a person who couldn't stop light-stringing until the sun was nearly set and the help was made to stand in front of the cactus while a 100-foot extension cord was run out and plugged in.

"Are they on?" I shouted down the driveway to the boys.

"Can we play football now?" they screamed back.

I took that to mean that, yes, the lights were on; yes, the effort was greatly appreciated; and, yes, Jesus would be coming down the street at any moment to heal my ruined and bloodied hands.

Pearl Harbor story retold by fewer each year, such as Mickey O

November 30, 2000

Mickey O is the genuine article, a tough, midsize man out of the old school, 79 and rail-thin, with a steel-spring grip and a pair of age-run tattoos on his forearms that he picked up in Honolulu for $7.50 apiece.

One is a snake-wrapped killing knife. The other is a hoochie-coochie dancer, and I guess it must have all seemed exotic to a kid out of a Pennsylvania mining town, an orphan put to work breaking coal when he was 10, a tough, hard-drinking guy who joined the Navy and found its 16-hour days easy by comparison.

It was fun, too, considering that it was 1941, with war threatening the United States and he and his buddies aboard the Pearl Harbor-based USS West Virginia blowing their $61 monthly wages on cards down in the double-hull, down so deep that officers never came looking, down so deep with each other they'd chip in a piece of the action for communal outings to Hotel Street.

It was there that Thomas "Mickey O" Michenovich met Violet Yung, a waitress at Wo Fats—a 19-year-old out of nowhere forging a friendship with a woman that he would know forever, or as close as we come to forever in one lifetime.

Later, he'd spend most of his years in Torrance working as a hod carrier, roofer and bartender. But back then he was a boy on the battleship West Virginia. And it's true that I'm early in telling his Pearl Harbor story, a death-and-infamy story of a kind that I will never tire of hearing firsthand, especially now, when the firsthand accounts are growing scarce.

But Mickey O has a reason for unfolding a long drawing of the West Virginia as it looked on December 7, 1941, a reason for recalling how the great ship sat outboard of the Tennessee and just ahead of the doomed Arizona at arm's length off Ford Island. The reason is the coming reunion and how a lot of guys that started the Pearl Harbor Survivors Association right here in the South Bay with Chapter One, are now too old and disconnected to get the news.

Mickey himself has been back these last eight years, and every year there are fewer and fewer men and more surprises. Like the last trip when he sat beside Jiro Yoshida, the Japanese pilot who launched the torpedo that struck his ship, the first of nine that hit the great ship above the armor, settling her into the mud bottom as the air outside filled with whistling shrapnel, as the water itself turned to fire and smoke that you can see still in old newsreels and in the memories of Mickey O.

He was shaving, a boy in underwear and clogs, thinking that a garbage scow had hit his ship. Then came eight more thumps that were fatal to 106 of his shipmates, not, ultimately, to the ship, which was eventually refloated. Unlike the Arizona, which is still there, still holding its young crew, still bleeding bunker oil into Pearl Harbor.

Mickey O tells the story without emotion. The product of a hard childhood, he'd already seen the Depression and men worked to death underground. A sneak attack seemed like more hard times to him as he took the order to abandon ship, seeing a friend cut in half by shrapnel as they ran under the forward gun turret, as 1,000 men jumped into flames and swam for Ford Island.

"That man in front of me was named Phil Reid, and if the 800 kilo bomb that hit the aft gun turret had exploded I would have ended like him. We would have gone up like the Arizona," he said. Only it didn't end right here. For two weeks after the fire and smoke stopped, he pulled bodies out of his ship. He helped remove his dead captain from the bridge and, only a few years ago, met that captain's now-aged children at a reunion where they thanked him.

Mickey O shook it off, "I don't try to think about it no more unless I go over to where we're having an all-sides reunion for everybody. Like last year when I went over to see Violet, who is 92 now and still getting around, and when I sat right beside Yoshida, the man who torpedoed us. This girl with him asked me in English how I felt and I told her, 'What happened happened, it's all over with.' "

He runs his hand over the ship drawing one more time, adding, "I don't feel bad or good about what happened, about what I saw of bodies below deck when we hauled them off in tarps. I volunteered to go back to the ship wearing borrowed clothes ... . It happened and it's over."

And so few can even remember.

That's the best darn pencil-holder juice can a dad could want

June 17, 2001

I always hit Father's Day with a "No, no, don't bother about me" on the lips. And I actually mean it, mostly. I'll take breakfast and a shirt, a goofy tie and some little thing made by a kid at school. I'm still using a pencil-holder juice can wrapped in colorful yarn given to me on Father's Day 1990, and I have kept it on display at home where I can see a collection of similar junk that was all presented like gold—which it is.

What I don't want is a restaurant brunch or anything expensive.

What I want are children being themselves, which is to say wishing me a happy day before getting into arguments over breakfast preparation, arguments that eventually work their way back to me in the form of "D-a-a-a-a-a-a-a-d ... !"

I'm supposed to hate this constant intrusion of children, but I don't because I know that, like glory, it is fleeting, growing up, heading elsewhere even as we live it.

Within this mayhem, my job is to smile and look happy. And at day's end, I always tell everyone how grateful I am for their efforts and how special they all made me feel. If I don't, I know that they will look hurt and ask me if I am grateful for the washed dishes, for the breakfast of fat-laden foods, for the weak coffee and pulpy juice.

So it's yes, yes, always yes.

And in there somewhere I will stop to consider the shadows of good men who travel with me still, the adopted traits that I wear even now like a too-large suit. Mostly what occupies me is how time stands perception on its head. Think how, in the same brain, we get to be small children offering treasures to fathers. Think how we tried to read the big, inscrutable, preoccupied beast as he sat in bed, his eyes always focused elsewhere.

I had a couple of fathers growing up. One gave me up for adoption, another took me as his own, which put me on the father/son track late. Missed was the bond I have with my son, with my daughters. Maybe too much is said about this. Maybe not enough can ever be said about where that bond comes from.

Listening to Sinatra at 2 a.m. with a new baby in your lap, explaining Frank's early career to a toothless, cooing baby because it's important, listening to tunes from his Capitol years, from his ring-a-ding-ding years, along the way explaining your own life to someone who can't understand a word you're saying. All just to stay awake while they drool, cry and nuzzle their warm baby smell into your neck until you become the same person.

While you become that person that you never thought that you could be, the guy in bed on a morning in June accepting presents, trying not to look elsewhere or think elsewhere when everything that is worth a damn is happening right there in front of you.

Still, it all comes back when you were, like them, dependent, at-the-mercy, vulnerable. The years of cards bought for stepdad, years of walking down to the 7-Eleven to buy a couple of boxes of .22 shells so the pair of us could plink away at cans and bottles. Not saying much, the old man going "How about that" when I'd accidentally hit something. Then, at the end of the day, extending his hand, "Thanks a lot."

And me thinking that this wasn't like television with the grandfatherly speeches and advice. Just a hand and the great way he made me feel when he introduced me as his son. This man who came to fatherhood, came to having a 7-year-old boy when he was 50 with no lead up, no blood children of his own to walk with, to feed, to know every fleeting moment of a young life as they pile up and vanish absolutely.

Just a man doing his best, like so many men who come to mind. Scoutmasters, my high school track coach Clarence Noe, a teacher or two, a priest, men in the truest sense, men who used the male aura that trailed in their wakes for good. Even if they didn't mean to do good, they did, filling in where there were blank spaces, saying not much, showing instead that maleness had nothing at all to do with violence and all to do with care, with doing not much together, with listening.

All of them come back to me on this day, that stepfather especially and those other fathers who never knew how important they were. These men whose importance I didn't see back then, couldn't possibly see because I was small and taking it all in, trying to invent myself.

But I can see it all now in a way that my children can't, making this less a day of thanks and more a day of endless gratitude passed along.

How to get rid of that lab-mice look without raising an eyebrow

September 2, 2001

I am not a vain man. Vain men spend money on hair plugs. I know a guy who dropped three grand on silicon calf implants because he always wanted big calves.

Who knew?

Certainly not me. I thought losing 20 pounds would have done him more good and it would have been cheaper.

All this I mention because I drove my wife last weekend to get her nails done. We were on our way somewhere, so I waited in a nail salon run by three industrious sisters out of the city formerly known as Saigon. I read Me, US, Myself, Me First and several other magazines whose primary job seems to be encouraging normal women to look like 18-year-old Euro models.

I was, by the way, the only male in the joint. A lone male taking in the peculiar vibe that comes from being the only one of his kind in an exclusively female place. And it's not that I mind the subtle mind-shift, this feeling that I am just a little bit toyed with and a lot in the minority.

And not a terribly popular minority at that.

What saved the situation is this other feeling I get, the attitude that any guy willing to wait for his wife in a place that smells like napalm couldn't be too much of a pig. So the nine women present just seemed to regard me in the usual way, like I was personally responsible for the entire male race never noticing what so many women spend so much time doing just for us. Or they say that things like nail painting are done just for us, for love, when it comes to pointing out that we didn't notice.

So sue us.

Still, there I was waiting like a saint when I realized that the bushy-browed gent my wife, a woman who regards the Saigon sisters as sisters, is talking about is none other than me.

"What?" I ask, looking across the room to where they titter.

"We were just saying that you could do with a waxing," replied my wife in the Scottish accent that somehow endears her to what she calls her "fellow foreigners." Don't ask me how that works but the tall, blond Scot somehow feels a sense of unity with all people not of this country born.

"A waxing of what?" I ask, a little angry at being pulled away from an article titled (I'm not making this up), "Twelve Ways To WOW Your Man In Bed!"

"Your eyebrows."

Yeah, well I have 12 suggestions for you right here.

"What's wrong with my eyebrows?"

"They look," she said, "like two lab mice."

Yeah, well I have another article here about wowing your man in the kitchen. . . . "When did you decide this?"

"Years ago," she joked to the amusement of the Saigon sisters and the other women in the napalm factory. Adding, "Her sister can give you a wax right now. Takes five minutes, lasts a month. You'll look like a million bucks."

Million bucks. Lasts a month? This sounded better than one of those TV ads for kitchen gadgets.

"Wait, I won't look like those old tweezed, orange-haired guys you see selling antiques?"

"Get one," she said. "It's on me."

Right then it was either go out and watch the oil leak out of my 33-year-old car or take the bet present in the eyes of all those women.

"Sure," I said, trying to sound like a tough guy on a lark while looking like a dork, following a Saigon sister into a cubical, to a lean-back chair where I sit, where she tells me, "This hurt a little," as she applies 5,000-degree wax to my virginal lab-rat brows and I wonder why women do this stuff.

Then some kind of fabric gets pressed into the goo. "This hurt," she said, yanking, bringing me back to the first time some coach pulled athletic tape off an unshaved ankle while offering those all purpose, soothing coachly words, "Wadda-ya, some kind a wuss?"

So I wasn't a wuss then. But now I am, a grown man wondering if he'd wind up looking like Gloria Swanson in "Sunset Boulevard," a man who realizes that he had taken a chance detour never traveled by any male member of his line and—come to think of it—damn few female ones.

What, in short, was I doing. Let me out of here. Panic was setting in, but one brow was done. I couldn't leave now. I was down for the count. Then it was over. Bada-boom!

"Big eyebrows no more," sister said.

I looked in a hand mirror like Peter Lorre in that movie where he awakens in a murderous mood from botched plastic surgery: "My face, what have you done to my face?"

But wait!

Hey, big eyebrows no more!

Better yet, nobody has noticed, especially not my male friends who wouldn't notice anything anyway. Which is just the way things should be.

There's less time to talk now, but the love speaks volumes

September 7, 2001

There should be no surprises here. I mean, how many times have I dropped a kid off at school. And how many of those were first days. The first-day concept only applying to the early years.

After that a kid would sooner admit to heading an opium tung than let you walk him into class.

But I'm a pro at this, the father of a late baby boy who, in what seemed like 10 minutes, somehow became a second-grader. I was doing first-days with his older sisters years before he was born.

Now I'm one of the older dads, doing a first-day on Tuesday with fresh-faced moms, moms in their 20s and 30s, moms who know one another from coffee and tennis.

I am the invisible one with a little boy who has been bumming on for three days about school, about how he doesn't really want to return, about how he'd like to take another week or so off so we can do stuff together.

Nothing specific, just stuff. You know, get in the car and go somewhere, talk a lot about nothing, maybe ride bikes or build something out of Lego blocks.

That's the funny thing about this late child, this boy. We spend a lot of time together, seeing ourselves in each other, recognizing that there is something important in this insane father-son thing.

It was something I missed. Sure, I had a stepfather, a good one. But there is something to be said about being there from the start. On the ground floor with two girls, then this boy, wondering for an improbable third time why newborns don't scream in terror at the sight of us masked and gowned, with hair growing out of our noses.

And what genetic trip wire makes even the most apprehensive parent-to-be fall so quickly and absolutely in love. One minute you don't know them from dirt, the next you're prepared to offer your heart for transplant if they need it.

My mother-in-law told me long ago, "Babies bring their love with them."

Believe me, I've seen sad situations where they don't. But mostly I have seen cases like mine, cases of love at first sight, cases where you madly snap 36 photos of a new baby in the exact same position, his little hands clenched, his tiny head in a stocking cap, swaddled in a blue blanket.

I remember how, on the day he was born, fretting that I would be 52 when he was 7.

Now I'm 52 and he's 7 and neither of us is complaining. In the evenings we go out together. He's on a Razor scooter and I'm jogging, answering questions that always seem to concern cars, motorcycles, space and life in general.

A life-in-general question is, "What if I marry someone who is really fat?"

I don't know the correct answer. So I say, "I don't suppose that it would matter if you loved her."

But he's already on to "Apollo 13," the movie, and how it just struck him that navigating a damaged spacecraft by keeping the Earth in the window isn't much different than what sailors did on wooden boats 1,000 years ago.

There is, of course, more time to talk like that during summers. There's no homework, no soccer or basketball, no lessons, no organized enrichment at all if you don't count the time we have together. Time that will be recalled in random moments to help explain this father and this boy to other little boys and girls undreamed of.

Now we're in the car together on our third first-day together. This time it's second grade across the SUV-jammed parking lot and down the hall. So many adults jammed into a space built for small children, the air thick with first-day assurances.

"Don't look so worried, I'll spring you at noon."

That's what I tell him as he arranges his supplies in his desk, blond head secreted behind the raised lid.

"How's my hair?" he whispers, the hair he spent 10 minutes arranging with Dep Sports Gel.

"You look fantastic."

"Give me one more hug before you go," he says.

Just one more.

Just when you think the violence is over, it's hardly begun

September 12, 2001

The kids found Riley in the driveway on Tuesday morning.

"Dad, we found a little dog!"

Indeed, Riley was cute with a tag around his muddy neck telling us his name, telling us he has a home, which we called.

Ten minutes later a mom—you know, a mom—appeared at the end of our long driveway in a gold minivan.

"Have you seen '101 Dalmatians?'" she asked my little boy. "Riley was in that movie." Then to me all serious, "Are your children going to school today?"

"Why wouldn't they?"

"You mean, you haven't heard?"

Is there some way to reverse the course of, "You haven't heard"? Because I hadn't heard at 7:15 on a morning that dawned bright for a change, the sun cutting beautifully through the upper branches of the big pine bordering my driveway and warming Riley, making steam rise off his rusty mutt coat.

"Heard what?" I ask, knowing that I have just asked to be shot between the eyes.

"Two airliners were crashed into the World Trade

Center and another into the Pentagon. They closed my son's school."

Ain't that just like life, people are surely dead/they closed my son's school. The yin and yang of existence. But they didn't close my son's school or my daughter's, so we drove with the radio bleeding information from NPR.

All of this beyond my boy, beyond my 15-year-old girl. They don't understand why anyone would want to kill so many people in a way that is impossible to bend the mind around.

Still, it is amazing how quickly the mind stretches itself to accommodate things so terrible that our worn-down language can't touch them.

Within 10 minutes of finally seeing the doomed jet heading into the World Trade Center, within 10 minutes of seeing the Pentagon in flames and those magnificent towers collapse, I had adapted to a new and dreadful reality.

Through some great synaptic twist we had all made the leap from the clearly impossible to the certain knowledge that people who hated enough to die for their hate, had crashed four commercial jets, utterly destroying two massive buildings and damaging a symbolic third.

Two shots to the head and one to the heart.

Somebody wants us dead, as always. Only this was organized by somebody with enough power and money to organize four suicide missions, spectacular cheap shots that sent people leaping to their deaths. And may the fools, of which there is never a shortage, who were convinced to do these things never find paradise in so many lives wasted.

Their lives as well, wasted. The tendrils of loss reaching across this small world. One life lost, a pebble tossed into a pond, the ripples spreading. Hundreds, thousands lost, a tidal wave.

As I write, it is only a few hours since the implausible

passed into reality. In that time my college daughter called from Tucson to tell us that our friends, Mike and Nancy Fusco landed at JFK at 6 a.m. in New York where Mike, a bond trader, has offices in the World Trade Center.

Only Mike was late, and is alive. This message passed on to my cell phone from Mike's daughter, Amanda, to our college daughter to us, the near miss making it real.

We soon had more news from a friend in San Francisco wanting us to know that a mutual friend had just lucked into a great job . . . in the World Trade Center.

It's all maybe and could have been at this point with smoke billowing off the tip of Manhattan, with its wonderful views of the Statue of Liberty and Ellis Island, the first place settled by the Dutch in an age when attack came by sea, from wooden ships. Smoking now—the scene begs for comparison—like Pearl Harbor.

The video repeats. An elegant airliner slams into the second tower.

All those people strapped to their seats, heading for Los Angeles or San Francisco and finding eternity instead.

Men and women exactly like us, moms and dads, children on board, on the ground, in those towers, in the pilot seats of four jets facing what kind of cold lunacy. Lunacy to be matched certainly by revenge that will, as always, miss its target—killing men, women, moms, dads, children, entire nations.

Violence never ends. It only escalates to breathtaking new heights.

The danger, always present in this country, of inflicting itself on fellow Americans who might resemble all the usual suspects.

Still, what comes to mind as Tuesday's sun passed back into gloom was an interview I saw many years ago, an interview in which Israel's former defense minister

Moshe Dyan was asked what to do with Ugandan strongman Idi Amin, a thug partially trained in Israel and unleashed on an innocent people.

What, the interviewer asked, do you do with such a man?

The former general didn't hesitate: "You kill him. You kill evil."

There are many steps in learning how to act at high school dances

December 11, 2001

There is but one rule for chaperoning a dance at a Catholic high school, a rule I learned from a tiny six-battery-flashlight-wielding nun many years ago.

It was a good rule for teen-age slow-dancers then and even more useful now.

The rule is this: Leave room for the Holy Spirit.

But even mentioning this horrified my 15-year-old daughter, who was already horrified by my telling her that I had been asked to chaperon her high school's Winter Ball.

"I only ask . . . no, I pray, that you won't try to be funny," she said, pushing the issue but not too hard since Saturday evening's Winter Ball also involves a new dress and a professional hair visit to Mr. Robert.

She also more or less demanded that I be nice to her date, a 6-foot-4, 15-year-old who was so polite and well-mannered that I decided not to be funny around him either—especially not after he called me "sir" six times.

Then there is the matter of the dance, a gathering of youngsters that seemed outwardly new and utterly different while inwardly remaining the same strange and complex mating ritual that baffled us.

This is because dances, then and now, involve girls.

If dances involved only boys, things would not be strange and complex because there is nothing strange and complex about boys putting each other in head locks and talking about sports.

Throw girls into the mix and you're suddenly facing something as baffling and mind-bending as the Middle East. Only they smell better. They look better, too, maybe better than girls ever looked before.

Would I be the first adult to observe that today's teen-age girls look like women? This while today's teen-age boys look, as always, like teen-age boys.

Their arms are too long, their skin spotty and every one of them—no matter how cool they think they are—looks like their moms dressed them with a suit a size too big so they'll grow into it.

Mixing godawful punch at a long table with the moms gave me a wonderful chance to watch everyone make their big entry into the gym. With every one so well groomed, the major difference between now and the old days being that girls these days are every bit as athletic as the boys.

Products one and all of vitamins, swim teams and many field sports, these kids seem to ripple rather than walk. Only all these sports have produced matchlessly beautiful girls who have no idea how to walk in tall shoes and evening gowns.

Not that it mattered after the formal photo-taking led directly to the 5,000-decibel, 90-degree gym, where all those youthful hormones and fine nerve endings set loose enough energy to power Kabul.

Little by little, dance by dance, any polish they walked in with vanished. Shoes and jackets came off, ties got a second wind as sweat bands and all the expensive hair-styles came undone.

Even from the punch table I could see that things

were getting outrageous because the faculty adviser guy seemed frightened and was operating well beyond his usual sphere of total control.

The girls were, of course, all dancing like Britney Spears in concert. Where, one has to ask, did our daughters learn to dance like that? But the strangest thing was how good they were at it, these girls who go to school in uniforms. And no need mentioning the Holy Spirit, which seemed to be alive in them and having a truly great time.

It was interesting to watch, what with the girls mostly dancing with each other and keeping up with the 180-beat-per-minute techno pop DJ. This while the boys appeared to be dancing obliviously to the Dave Clark Five.

Later the faculty guy transferred me from punch to the side door, where my middle-age parental invisibility allowed me to see the absolute truth of this tribal ritual. The truth is that we get to be kids for only a short time, and for a short time we get to have actual fun.

Then, if all goes according to the grand plan, we wind up serving punch and guarding the side door while our children have fun.

Cleaning out the shelves of kids' books stalls as memories take over

July 11, 2004

I needed to get rid of the kid books, two entire shelves that I winnowed down as our last child grew away from silly stories printed over bright pictures that—now that I look at the price tags on these things—cost a fortune.

Some of them are 20 years old and they were expensive even then. Still, there comes a time when we must part with things, especially books because books take up shelf space and we all know that shelf space is worth its weight in wood and the time it took to assemble these things.

In my case, it took two entire days using special skin-slicing Ikea tools. It was a long ago Thanksgiving and I remember it distinctly because my mother spent the entire assembly time nagging me about the pitfalls of buying cheap stuff. Now here I was, with the mother long gone and the children all grown or getting there, culling the vast collection. Already donated is the Sesame Street collection and all books featuring little girls, horses, little girls and princes and ballerinas. Also missing are counting, letter and handwriting books, all the basic education stuff that we pored over like code breakers.

When I sat down on the floor to box the hundred or so

remaining books I figured 10 minutes work and I'd have room finally for important adult material like expired Thomas Guides and all the classics I've been meaning to read.

But it took maybe 30 seconds to see why I hadn't already ditched this stuff. For here was *Little Bear*, by Else Minarik and Maurice Sendak inscribed to our eldest daughter from her best friend, "Brian, Chanukah 1985."

"Do you want to keep this?" I asked the pretty 21-year-old as she passed.

She was horrified. "Brian gave me that!" Then, sitting cross-legged beside me, "This is the one where Mother Bear makes Little Bear a hat. We're keeping it."

"How about *The Digging-est Dog*, by Al Perkins?"

"NO!" screamed the recent college grad. "This is where Duke the dog has to be taught how to dig by the little boy. ... Read it. She hands it to me and waits for the much-loved lines of doggie internal monologue, "I dug up daisies. I dug up seeds. I dug up a fence. I dug up gates. I dug up the garden of Mrs. Thwaites."

Children love to see animals doing bad things, even this big child sitting beside me saying, "I love *Hop On Pop*: 'Day play. We play all day. Night night we fight all night.'"

"Now this," she said, handing me a book that I don't need to read because I know it better than what I just wrote.

"I am Sam," it begins and, don't you know, he does not like green eggs and ham, damn! And neither do I because I spent years attempting to skip pages at bedtime only to be reeled back in like big daddy fish and threatened with a sleep boycott.

Try it, go ahead you newly minted parents and you, too, will see that you will come to hate it on a train, in the night, during the day and any other time you'd rather be engaged in adult play, play, play.

Then she decided that we can't possibly part with *The Jester Has Lost His Jingle* by David Saltzman, a fine young man who grew up on the Palos Verdes Peninsula, graduated Yale and wrote this amazing book before dying of Hodgkin's disease 11 days short of his 23rd birthday.

Next comes the obscure *The Old Man of Lochnagar*, by His Royal Highness The Prince of Wales ... really. It's about an old Highlander who lives near Scotland's Lochnagar. We visited the place once and our daughters spent an hour peering into its freezing water until they actually saw the Old Man; kilt, hairy knees and all.

Also placed on the save list was a fantastically illustrated *Rumpelstiltskin*, by Paul Zelinsky, everything by Beatrix Potter and *Dinosaur Roar*, by Paul and Henrietta Strickland.

Finally, the books to be lost numbered two, one badly used coloring book and a sad pop-up book with four missing pages.

"You'll need these for our kids," said my daughter who, only yesterday, was a kid herself.

At college send-offs everywhere, dads mask emotions with muscle work

September 28, 2004

The division of labor outside the college dorm was sexist and heartbreaking and happening for many after a lemming-drive up the I-5 to Davis with bikes on racks and dads wheeling back-heavy SUVs.

In the IHOP on the other side of the Tejon Pass, my freshman girl said, “It’s like building a house in Malibu and never getting to live in it.” The room was full of early-morning eaters, full of parents just like me and daughters and sons just like my daughter who pretty much nailed it with that jokey remark about building something almost wonderful in children and then not being able to enjoy them.

The dozen UC Davis-bound kids in the IHOP represented, in lifetime upkeep costs, the annual GNP of Luxembourg. And I’m just talking clothes, shoes, books, Halloween costumes, food, birthday cakes, Brownie uniforms, doctor’s visits, orthodontics, bikes, scooters, baseball gloves and those little elastic hair bands that girls leave everywhere.

Unmeasurable is the emotional investment, the 18 years of unpaid labor, the diapering, walks, the running out in the middle of the night for infant Tylenol, the crying-baby sleep deprivation until you see the face of Jesus in the window come sunup, the sad mornings at preschool when they don't want you to leave, the afternoons at preschool when THEY don't want to leave, the fears and insecurity before kindergarten, the fears before grades 1-7, the fears before high school and now the fears before college.

That is to say, the emotional investment doesn't end at the dorm entrance, not for me, not for any parent who did all the above out of duty and love and insanity.

And here we all are, in middle age looking depleted in our sports clothes, performing a ritual that nobody really wants to perform.

We've turned squalling babies into interesting adults, more or less. Now we are compelled to leave them, to replace love with checks and to hear of their lives long-distance in what might be seen as a kind of institutionalized penance, a heart-rending moment where—lacking true models of standard operating behavior—we revert to type.

Working under a strict parking-enforcement deadline, dads do the muscle work, hustling stuff on dollies up ramps, into the dorm lobby, up elevators and into rooms that are more apartment-complex-like than old-line dorm. The stuff coming is sometimes extreme, living proof that college is not what it was when we were young. Refrigerators are usual, so are microwaves, though the nearest food market—and why is this so often the case around college campuses?—is a mile away.

My favorite was the guy wheeling in an outsize flat-screen TV and a rack of supporting electronics. There were also nice desk chairs, lamps, computers, DVD collections, CD collections, all of it unfolding from SUVs like the contents of a clown car.

While dads muscled the junk and siblings bobbed to music on earphones, mothers fussed with big white plastic bags from Bed Bath & Beyond. Through open doors, I could see them zipping on the sanitary mattress covers, laying down clean sheets and rugs, unfurling quilts, organizing toiletries, spraying Lysol, lots of Lysol, for boys and girls and verbal warnings tumbling out windows. Moms mention sheet changing and towel washing, dads want to go over the bike lock and chain one more time.

"Keep the chain as far from the ground as possible," I tell my daughter, being no different than any other guy. "It makes it more difficult to use ..."

"... bolt cutters on it," she pipes in, finishing my sentence. "You've told me." But no matter how many times I go over things, it kept coming back to this moment being several moments past time for leaving. So we hug, and she promises that she won't run after the car as I drive off.

Then she runs after the car for a few steps as I accelerate. In the mirror, I could see her smile, turn and walk away.

Cavity and the senior menu offer a peek at mortality on eve of birthday

October 8, 2004

I just broke a tooth. Actually it was only that portion of a molar not filled in with silver, mercury and—who knows—plutonium. I have this thing because I grew up in the 1950s when our wise elders were hotly debating fluoride and other precious bodily fluids.

My kids got fluoride and zero cavities. I have five, two of them quite large, one of them paining me on this, the eve of my birthday.

Sure, this dental destruction could have happened when I was 30, but it didn't. It happened now, two weeks after an IHOP waitress on the I-5 told me, "You can save money if you order off the senior menu." She pointed to a legend at the menu's bottom, "Seniors—55 and over." Congratulations, boy. You saved three bucks. Next it will be early-bird dinners.

But back to a tooth first drilled when I was 13. Thirteen! We got history, this tooth and me. While the rest of our body tissue replaces itself, teeth stay on as original equipment and fixing this one means calling my dentist and begging an appointment because the exposed filling feels rough and my tongue won't leave it alone.

What's worse, it broke while I was eating a veggie

burger. You know what that is? It's food substitute. It's soybeans made to look and taste almost like meat. But it wasn't real meat. It wasn't a T-bone with steak fries. It was veggie burger and veggie salad, what my wife's Scottish granny disdainfully called "rabbit food." I'm breaking teeth on rabbit food.

Next I'll be haunting malls, looking for the perfect frozen yogurt with a senior discount.

Weird stuff always happens near my birthdays, little cosmic reminders. A guy I used to work with, Stan Allison—the very picture of life—died the other day. Three years younger than me and a hundred pounds heavier, boom, Stan is gone. Natural causes. Then Rodney Dangerfield.

I met the man years ago in Culver City when he was making one of those celebrity-jammed Lite beer commercials. The Packers' fearsome Ray Nitschke was there, too. They're both gone now, along with Gordon Cooper, Mercury astronaut, free spirit and boyhood hero.

Gone, "I get no respect," gone the meanest football player ever, gone the ever youthful Gordo Cooper.

Gone too many friends.

My grandmother, Carmella Moreno, lived to be 87. One night she ate a huge meal with red wine, went to bed and died. Nana, we'd call her. Many Italians call their grannies that. One day Nana was talking about the six children she lost in childbirth in the old country and about losing her husband and an entire neighborhood of men and women that were once her life.

"What are you going to do?" she sighed, pretty much summing up how I felt when my tooth broke as I ate a food-like substance that she wouldn't have allowed into her house.

Meanwhile, my son has been asking me if I am looking forward to my birthday mainly because he always looks forward to his. He counts days like a soldier. Me, I'm trying to hold them off, trying to appreciate the moment and enjoying the occasional shock of just being alive.

Driving through Big Sur or maybe walking out to the parking lot like I did the other night when the coastal fog glowed with obscured sunlight, it just hits me—these dopey mawkish moments—as wonderful.

And my daughter's roommate-to-be, the girl who somehow went over a cliff during a party in Santa Barbara and lay unconscious for two weeks, woke up Saturday, the day after my son's entire Catholic school prayed for her.

It was a miracle!

It wasn't a miracle.

It was just nature and I'm not the first person to suspect that all such words hint at the same nearly indescribable thing encompassing pretty animals, the talent of ballplayers, comedians and astronauts and the fragile, dangling-for-a-moment life of a splendid 18-year-old girl who may come out of this whole.

Meanwhile, my tooth is broken and I'm turning 56 as the ranks tumble before me, as they should.

Forced to play AYSO's ratings game, but without very much enthusiasm

November 2, 2004

Calling a collection of 11-year-old boys a team is stretching it. Yes, we're playing soccer and, yes, they are all wearing the same jersey, but this is not the 1961 Packers. Nor am I Vince Lombardi.

For starters, I'm too tall and they are too short.

Plus they have an annoying habit of watching planes fly over or dogs running along the sidelines or singing to themselves when they should be concentrating on making me the greatest AYSO coach in history.

That's another thing. They don't care if we ever get the soccer version of the Lombardi Trophy. In fact, I'm not terribly certain that they care all that much about winning. You see, not only is this not the 1961 Packers, this is not 1961. Kids today have things to do. They have tests to take, instruments to learn, plays to act in, books to crack, Scouts to swear, video games to play and schools to attend.

They are, in short, the prisoners of paranoid parents who want the best for them. Though I'm not always certain that we are actually doing our best with the overload.

As if getting them to all shoot at the same goal isn't enough, AYSO each year expects me to perform the truly onerous rite of player ratings.

I first encountered this system that is supposed to order kids from the best to least when I was coaching my son and his fellow 5-year-olds. On the rating sheet I was asked to judge babies prone to seeking out their mother's laps during games by their ball skills, understanding of the game, speed, aggressiveness (I had a scary biter that year) and attitude.

Not being a hard guy, I looked down the list of cherubs and gave them all the maximum score. Figuring that this was some kind of report card, I didn't want parents thinking badly of their tiny jocks.

I turned in my sheet and got maybe 6 feet from the coaches' tent when somebody yelled, "Is this yours?" Seriously, if I wanted to be talked to in that tone of voice I'd just stay at home with my family. "You can't do this!" the man added.

As with so many things in life I had to decide, would I beat this fellow with a large stick or would I politely ask him what he was talking about?

As you can see by an absence of columns written from jail, I chose the latter. Here is where I learned that ratings are used to organize the following year's teams. If I rate all my players high, that means that each one of them will be assigned as the top kid on one of next year's teams.

And the truth was, most of my kids couldn't find the ball with both feet. From then on the job, unpaid and thankless in a conventional sense, has included ratings that grow more serious with each passing year. This last weekend, as a horrid political season stumbled toward its end, I attended a meeting with my fellow coaches, hardly any of whom were born in the United States.

It sounds like a setup for a bad joke with a Scot, a German, a Russian, an Englishman and a Frenchman talking about the massive importance of judging small boys.

Important or not, it's still difficult. That is to say, looking at names on paper doesn't make me think ball handling and speed. What I think of is how one kid does a great impression of Dr. Evil or how another boy's mom combs his unruly hair into place before games, then turns away because she can't bear the suspense of play.

One of my forwards is from a group home and all I see there is a kid happy to be in a place where the bad stuff that happened to him can be forgotten in the exuberance.

Only now they are teetering on the edge of being something bigger and more quantifiable. In many ways, this is the last year they will be allowed to play like little boys and without the relentlessly increasing pressure that accompanies age onto the athletic field.

Still, I classify and winnow because I don't want some coach next year to think that he's getting a 9 when what he's actually getting is a gift beyond measure.

Little League bleacher show aside, parents are there for the kids

March 4, 2005

On a sodden Saturday morning I'm sitting on metal bleachers beside a hairy mumbling dad who arrived bathed in Jovan Musk For Men. He's talking tax returns. Yeah, that's it, taxes and very bad words in English and Russian.

On the other side of the backstop the Little League coach has our boys lined up for the sportsmanship and game-basics lecture.

That's what the lads need, basics—batting basics, catching basics, being-nice basics. And the kids, 12 of them in new Chicago Cubs caps and muddied cleats, are devoting their severely compromised attention spans to a large mutt attempting to mate with a small poodle in center field.

The only thing apparently more interesting than the dogs are the owners, two of our own parents, frantically yanking leashes and screaming at each other. To me, this is enveloping action, the opening scene that past experience tells me will sum up the entire upcoming season of people-watching. You see, kids might play soccer or basketball, but nothing beats the slower drum of baseball, a clock-free game that allows hours of idle time.

C'mon, it's a sport where players eat nachos during a game of wait and wait longer, a game often interrupted by as many as 10 straight seconds of action. In between, I watch. Not the game, the parents and the peculiar dynamics of parents who are, face it, kids who have just gotten taller.

When 13-year-old girls, softball players, take the opposite field I can hear the eyes of our boys click from the dogs to girls pulling ponytails out of holes cut in the backs of pink baseball caps. At ages 9 through 11, they mostly do not know exactly why the girls seem so mysterious, so unknowable with their giggles and failure to even look in their scrawny-kneed direction. Still, the boys are enthralled.

"Gentlemen!" demands the coach, as half the boys look over their shoulders.

Nothing back there but parents, which is a real cavalcade of frailty.

Watching evaporating water hovering foglike just above the field I recall past parental moments. Take the 40ish assistant coach, his beautiful, young blond wife and how his equally beautiful, blond 40ish former wife would show up and sit with her replacement, looking for all the world like an older sister.

They even dressed alike and often brought their dogs, two identical golden retrievers, two nearly identical women in Spandex pants rooting for son and stepson and both getting kissed on the cheek by the boy at game's end. Luckily, the old wife's new husband didn't look anything like the old husband. He was younger and even better looking and they were impossible not to watch in their successful parting and re-pairing.

Not so with many other parents, the divorced ones who sat rooting for the same kid from different ends of the bleachers, the former lovers who couldn't look each other in the eye, let alone engage in civility.

Then there were the marrieds, happy or miserable in ways not unique.

There were the suited power couples sitting side by side while engaging in cell phone abuse with others. And the lawyer dads, as always, pacing the third-base line like wolves, absorbed in phone calls, their faces mixtures of anger and angst as their wives appear in massive SUVs, perfect and expensive.

Always there is anger, pent up and not. Two years ago a weedy little guy from an opposing team came unhinged, having to be restrained when he came after one of our dads, a former semi-pro football player with 20-inch arms. Our dad didn't take the bait. Nobody died.

Which is understandable because we are all children, only big now and entangled, flawed in our ways, good in our ways and—most important—out there for the kids, like we are supposed to be.

Many flag-waving, freedom-loving Americans are overlooking one thing

March 13, 2005

Touch me! Good Scout that I am, I walked right into my local fire station, right into a shaky cardboard voting booth and cast my vote for some guy who bored me comatose.

I even took my son with me, which is something I did with his sisters before him. You see, I have this weird idea that nearly everything they are going to learn about family values, community and the thin line of civility separating us from the dirtbags who think that our Constitution goes a bit too far is going to come from their parents.

For years I was the guy in the voting booth with 10 legs; that's one perplexed dog, two small daughters and dad. Know what I got from those early-morning, before-school, get-up-early walks between parked fire engines? I got a nifty little sticker saying, "I voted." Best of all, I got two girls who now vote. I got two girls who are bewildered by friends who don't.

Not that their friends are unusual. Most of us don't vote.

Everybody has an opinion, of course. Everyone feels passionately about absolutely everything.

Meanwhile, three-fourths of L.A.'s 1.47 million registered voters routinely don't bother to vote

Of course, the only thing at stake on this day was the Mayor's Office, a position so unimportant in a nation-size city that 100,000 fewer voters turned out than four years before.

Meanwhile, in smaller cities all over the county, candidates are winning offices based on numbers that look like they are out of student council elections.

Why is this the case? Good question. And it just so happens that I have been listening to mealy-mouthed excuses from nonvoters for most of my life. Mind you, I'm a bit of an eccentric in this matter because I came up in a neighborhood of ward bosses and peasant solidarity, a place where voters realized before they took out citizenship papers—even before they learned to speak English—that they could indeed throw the bums out.

To them, voting was power, the very thing they had come here lacking absolutely. Even though they came looking for a buck, discovering a one-man, one-vote system seemed a great gift.

That's the background I have to stifle when I hear the excuses and the shameless conviction with which these excuses are delivered. It's always the same.

Shall I list them?

"One vote doesn't matter." Ask Al Gore and Richard Nixon. What kind of special idiot actually believes that his vote and world view—even when filtered through the nutty electoral college—is worthless and says so?

How about, "All those guys are crooks!" Sure, that might be the case because the people in question are politicians, an occupation some might rank just above prostitution. But, like democracy itself, it's what you got and what you got is better than whatever second-rate tyrannical system you've been spared for over two centuries.

Neither should we forget the much-used "It doesn't matter." While such a philosophy might score points among French existentialists, the fact remains, it matters a lot or it matters a lot if you happen to be interested in where we kill and who dies, where the highway money goes, how the schools are funded and which candidates mention the word "God" most often.

I'm just tired of hearing these excuses because that's all they are, excuses for an ignorant shirking of an act that is more responsibility than right.

I've been around a little and I've never seen another country where so many people wave so many flags with such single-minded belligerence, where God and country and fighting and dying for our freedoms—and singing about these terrible things in bellicose country tunes—is followed up by exercising the right not to vote.

Really, unless you're actually doing the fighting and dying or voting (that simple, timeless, priceless and painless act), maybe you should just shut up about your precious freedoms because you don't deserve them.

Dude, I got a totally rockin' stereo system for free—sort of

December 1, 2005

Never go to a big electronics store on the first big shopping day of the big shopping season. Actually, don't go anywhere at all between Thanksgiving and Christmas unless forced to do so. Unfortunately, I have attained an age where I can be forced to do things against my will by the very people I spent years forcing to do things against their wills.

And this wasn't an enriching piano lesson. This was a mobbed, soul-crushing electronics store where I was taken because I had yet to use the gift card my three children gave me a year ago to buy a car CD player.

Luckily, the kid running the store's CD-player section had a pierced nose and a firm grasp of exactly what I needed. And what I absolutely needed was a 1,200-watt amplifier and speakers the size of those once used by Led Zeppelin to deafen a generation.

"What kind of music do you like?" nose-puncture asked.

"Books on tape mostly," I replied.

"That's like, what, reading?"

"Yeah, like words."

"Like, you need something smaller."

Like, I also didn't mention that I had to hold off installation until I finished the 17 cassette memoirs of Ulysses S. Grant.

This is how I wound up in an infantile game of choose-and-frown. I'd choose a CD player from a wall-mounted selection of players and the kid would shake his head no. It seemed to be some kind of silent subterfuge based on my unspoken trust in a sullen but helpful child that I had known for 30 seconds.

"This one looks good," I'd say, based upon nothing at all, because all the pulsing, lit-up units looked like they had been pirated from alien spacecraft.

"No," his look would tell me as we went from brand to brand until we got the exact one that he and all his friends use because it's good, wonderful, kind and—I don't know—generous, and I can't for the life of me recall what the brand is.

"Couldn't you just have pointed this one out?" I asked.

Again with the head shake, "Store policy." Ah, store policy. But how do I know store policy doesn't include hooking idiots like me up with bad CD players?

"Seriously, dude, this is the best," the dude confided. "And it comes with free installation."

Well, it so happens that free is very close to my favorite price. But I naturally needed a few additional items for a few extra bucks, things like a wiring harness and a dashboard customizing kit. It said so right on the computer screen. I also needed the ability to imagine why the guy I bought my Wrangler from ordered it with super good speakers and no CD player? Did he think that tapes were the wave of the future? More to the point, did I actually need the $29 extended warranty for something that will probably be stolen because my car's roof and sides are made of plastic and zippers?

"You know that you'll break it," the youngest child—a son—said, not allowing me to fully digest how installation is free unless the installer decides that it should cost $50.

Right then is when my name boomed across the giant store's giant PA system: "Bogert, we have your lost child!"

"You lost a child?" asked the kid who was ringing me up.

Actually, I'd like to lose this lost child at times. Specifically, at times like this because she is 19 and possessing a badly bent sense of humor. This kid is smart, too, but intellectually preoccupied and if she couldn't find us after wandering off to look at a nearby clothing store it wasn't because she forgot which department we were in. No, it was because she hadn't noticed in the first place.

We found her up front. The 19-year-old guard who had called for us stopped hitting on her just long enough to continue this piece of public performance art, saying, "Sir, you need to keep better track of your kids."

You need to be a parent to fully understand it when I say that I wish I could. I honestly do.

Baseball's value always has been what you pass along to your son

August 9, 2007

Walking into Dodger Stadium on Sunday afternoon, into that wide expanse of technicolor green, I was reminded of the day I took my son to his first game. I remember his eyes when he took in the vastness of the place and the crack of bats in the spring air.

Mainly what I remember is that we were two hours early. So I got the time wrong. Sue me. But what's the difference when you want to show a 4-year-old the reason why a game played by grown men dressed like little boys is so otherworldly sublime, Zen-like and cool?

Being practically the only people in the park is probably what attracted the video crew, four guys working for the Dodgers organization who followed us into the grandstand, where my son and I stood looking down at the field, at batting practice, at a scene as timeless as any on Earth.

What I said next didn't originate with me. But I wasn't kidding either, or even making an attempt at irony when I told him, "This is why they call ballparks cathedrals."

"Wow," he said, which is what little boys are supposed to say when they see a major league park for the first time. I said the same thing in 1961 when I walked into little Yankee Stadium for a spring training game.

"You should see Wrigley Field," my far more worldly Chicago friend, Ward Brisick, replied.

Yeah, I should. I knew it instantly. But I really thought that seeing anything greener than that, anything better edged and more laden with talent (Maris, Mantle, Berra and Ford were in the lineup) and tradition than that would surely take my breath away. And that vision never ceased to push me right back into boyhood.

Later, in New York, Atlanta, San Francisco and L.A., it was the same. Like walking into St. Peter's.

So there I was holding my son's soft hand and saying this timeless dad thing and it could have been 1910 or 1950 for all the difference there was in that verdant scene, in that dirt diamond, when one of the video guys-shouts, "That was fantastic!"

I am, of course, a little miffed because I hate cameras pointing at me and partly because I was having a meaningful momement.

"Would you mind doing it again, only with your son on the left?" asks the video guy, who is maybe 25 and acting like the world is his to direct.

Also at work was the now universally accepted belief that we should all be honored to do anything for a camera. "Could you just walk in and say the same thing again, only with your son on your left?"

Reluctantly, we did it. Only the kid moved to my right. So we did it again and again the kid moved to the right finally saying, "I don't want to stand there, it's too close to the steps."

Thankfully, our chance to work free for whatever billionaire that owned the team was over. But it was the beginning of something bigger, the root of his Little League involvement, of baseball card collecting, of game-going and the sweet agony of picking out just the right mitts and bats on preseason Saturday afternoons.

For my son, and don't ask how this strange desire bypassed me completely, it also started him on the road to memorizing all the statistics stretching from last Sunday afternoon's game against the Diamondbacks back to—I don't know—the very first game of rounders played by British troops on some New England common in 1777.

To him—to legions of boys not diverted by foreign sports—the numbers attached to every player, their every RBI, every home run, every error transforms a slow agrarian game into a time machine, into a connection between fans long gone and the living, between those who ever played and loved the game to those as yet unborn who will someday occupy a father's lap and hear him enthuse like a child over pitchers and power hitters remembered like saints.

It's all simple grace and simple game, a short reprieve from the world out there, the world without rules or order, the world of woeful statistics and death-struggles.

"Enjoying the cathedral?" my son asked during a sixth-inning daydream.

He was making fun of me ... and he wasn't making fun of me at all.

Celebrating a child's 21st birthday seems nothing short of a miracle

August 31, 2007

It used to be that men were not allowed the pleasure of witnessing childbirth. On the contrary, males in the pre warm-and-fuzzy centuries remained at a grateful remove from a natural and miraculous process that is equal parts knife fight and that scene from "Alien." You know the scene.

I will never forget the day a friend described for me the birth of his first child in the hippie farmhouse he shared with some hairy people. I was 18 at the time and of the opinion that men were supposed to nervously inhale Lucky Strikes while babies hatched in a distant room.

Anyway, this guy, whom I saved on that very night when I stupidly and reflexively stopped a broken glass that somebody was trying to jab into his face, told me how after his commune-mates watched his wife deliver, all ate a small piece of placenta like it was a sacrament.

After throwing up, I resolved to never have children, especially children that came into this world as babies and especially not with any woman who would demand that I dine on jettisoned body parts.

No man could blame me for such resolution. And if he does, he isn't being honest. Either that or he's too young to recall a time when men were not expected to share in all this joy.

But back to childbirth. By the time my spouse talked me into having a child it was already a given that I would participate in the glorious event down to wearing blue pajamas, face mask and hair net.

Then this transformation took place. Actually, it was more transmogrification or epiphany or one of those other words that inadequately describe a complete makeover not involving a lobotomy. One minute I was standing there in a delivery room wondering what would happen if I didn't like this baby. And, more importantly, what would happen if I passed out.

Luckily, I had spent some time in a small Southern town covering gunshot and knife murders. By comparison, birth was almost tidy.

Then our first child popped into life head first.

One minute it was, "I hate babies." The next it was, "Doctor, if she needs a heart or a brain or anything, she can have mine!"

Call it love at first sight. Call it amazing three times over as I experienced the exact same angst and the exact same change of heart, going from "What if I don't like this child?" to "I really like this child!" in a nonce.

After that all the usual things happened, all the standard life milestones. First step, first day of school, first date, first everything. Seriously, I'm such a sucker for this stuff I even like hearing about other people's children. It's the same with weddings, I never seem to tire of them or the reaffirmation they toss into the face of bleak reality.

The point of this being how the other day was my middle child's 21st birthday. It seems nearly impossible to me to think that I first wrote about this child on a portable computer the size and weight of a tactical nuclear device. Resting the thing on my sleeping wife's hospital bed, I spent a dark night writing about instantaneous love and about what it was like to gaze into the glassy little eyes of a child born five weeks early with a space alien head and some appendages.

During this girl's first 2 a.m. on Earth I found myself in a hospital nursery alone with all 4 pounds of her on my chest, an imperceptible weight sucking on a bottle the size of something designed for a chimp. She sucked endlessly, producing only minuscule air bubbles that would disappear like hope vanishing. Only the kid survived somehow. Actually, not somehow. The kid had a will of steel and an idea, built in, that "no" was only a starting place for negotiations.

Into this great progression of events came her second birthday, came a robust little girl with tangled hair and mismatched clothing opening presents and proclaiming, "It's my birthday!" She was, of course, differentiating herself from her beautiful big sister and from everyone else on this planet. This was Rachael's birthday and nobody else's. But to me it was music, the sweet song of a child who finally had a firm grip on life.

And somehow all the glorious good times and bad times came and went. And somehow, after a year in Europe and entering her senior year in college, that little girl I wrote about so long ago became 21.

It is, of course, common enough that I feel this way, common enough that a child turns 21. Come to think of it, every second of all those years were just breathtaking, regular run-of-the-mill miracles.

Seeing the world through a teen can be eye-opening

September 7, 2007

I'm neck deep in back-to-school week.

On top of that my 13-year-old eighth-grader asked me to proofread a poem assigned to him on the first day of English class. The first day! The poem was titled "I Am" and in reading it I discovered that he'd someday like to have two sons and live across the street "from where I used to live when I was a kid." Which, of course, is the house he currently lives in because he is still that kid.

Oh, and he wants to name his sons Van Helsing and Mickey Mantle Bogert.

"If my wife and I have a third son, we'll name him Tom Brady Bogert," he wrote.

Van Helsing is, of course, the fictional vampire hunter while Mantle is The Mick and Brady is the New England Patriots QB. But more on these fictional sons and fictional wife later.

Now back to back-to-school week, Catholic school style. Which is to say, the school needs money, as always! Actually, they need it all at once. Within the next few days, I know from long experience, I will receive information on the coming jog-a-thon, a yearly tradition that generates more money than a McDonald's franchise.

There also will be announcements for the sale of the following items: See's Candies, Cub Scout popcorn, Girl Scout cookies and God forbid I should start a year without a letter warning me that my son also will be selling Sally Foster gift wrap, which is more costly than the costly skin of a new BMW.

Every year we buy six rolls of the stuff, which means that for the past 14 years one or another of our offspring have trundled out a single paltry box of wrapping paper on pickup day while other kids have their parents back in SUVs to carry away their orders.

But best of all is the announcement for the annual back-to-school gray-meat-burgers-on-wet-bread dinner. Every year we go and sit at long folding tables on the playground and make small talk with far younger parents who always seem to be talking about having second and third kids or buying new BMWs with lacquered skins as smooth as their own, as smooth as Sally Foster gift-wrap.

Then there's the sudden advent of flag football, a sport that must be closely watched by all parents if it is watched at all, if you have any heart at all. That's because if I don't watch the game—if only for a moment I should talk to some mom about the wonderfully scandalous behavior of another mom occupying a chair just out of earshot—my son will make the play of his life and I will miss it.

And should I miss it, we won't be able to analyze his moves, combing through them like airplane wreckage, until they come to resemble in the retelling something as sublime and beautiful as a ballet.

I don't know exactly why we do this but it might have something to do with how we are both males and victims of the sports we have adopted to take the place of hunting, gathering and the once holy passing of seasons.

Somewhere in this glut of activity, when I think that

I am not ready to do it all again, it occurs to me that this is the last time I will do this, the last new year at this school, my last year with a 13-year-old boy going on as only a boy his age can about pro and college players that weigh in like circus elephants.

Now back to the poem, which I quote here in selected snippets with permission of the author and quote at all because there is still something endearing about these last passing days of boyhood.

It begins, "I am a liberal because I like being different from everyone else." OK, so he's my kid, but I didn't know that he thought of himself as a liberal or thinks of being liberal as something distinctive. After all, many liberals spend a great deal of time trying to convince conservatives that they aren't liberal at all.

He continues, "I wonder why we don't try harder to save the planet we live on."

Then, and this is the kind of statement that soon won't come easily, "I cry if I think about the night my dog Cymbre died."

I wasn't, however, ready for this line: "I understand that love exists and that it is just the greatest feeling and that it's one of the very few true things in the world."

I'm surprised because most men spend decades getting to the nature of true things. That is, if they ever get there at all.

And this: "I dream that one day I will be married to a beautiful woman, a smart and funny woman who loves me and that we will both love each other more than the day we met. I dream that we have two boys" (the above-mentioned ones).

Then "I try to be a nice brother, friend and son. I hope that I will get into a good college and get a good job that I like and make enough money doing it." He concludes, "I am a liberal and like being different."

Only he's not so different in all the longing that goes

with being 13 and all the desires that go with being a human being. With these coming amid the popcorn, cookies and all the other things that dilute us and wind up making dreams of our dreams.

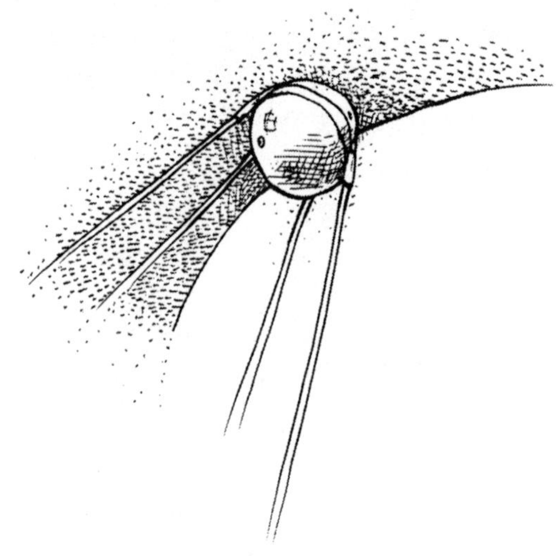

Anniversary of Sputnik launch recalls era of Cold War craziness

October 2, 2007

Sputnik!

It was a wondrous word, a terrifying word turned Cold War cliche and space trivia question. It means "fellow traveler." And it spelled national defeat to an American public so saturated with nonspecific Cold War dread we couldn't discern between a harmless chrome Russian basketball in space and the real threat.

The only thing that we were certain of when the Russians took that first flying leap into space was this: Our scientists would save us.

If you were raised on the era's science fiction claptrap, you knew that some pipe-smoking elder in a white smock would save us. Sure, it was a lie written by a guy at Republic Pictures. But it did give us a comforting blind spot, the one where we can't see that science can't solve most of our problems. That and how scientists are people like us, only with beards, who go to church on Sundays and pray to God that somebody will figure this mess out.

And the world-enthralling mess back on October 4, 1957, was Sputnik, a scientific advance of such mythical proportions it caused then Sen. Lyndon Johnson to remark, "I for one do not plan to go to sleep by the light of a Russian moon."

In my household, Sputnik rocketed to an even lower level. When I asked my mother about what they meant by an artificial moon, she replied, "When you look in the sky you'll see two moons."

I should explain to anyone under a certain age that the American people knew about as much as the Russian people when it came to artificial moons.

Know what Sputnik did? It went beep-beep like the tedious Road Runner of Siberia. Later these things would be called artificial satellites, then just satellites with thousands of them littering low-Earth orbit.

Which leads back to the real problem that almost everybody missed in 1957. The news wasn't the silver beeping ball, it was the monstrous Russian rocket that lifted it.

Putting this thing into space meant that the Ruskies could also drop a thermonuclear device on Torrance. OK, so our leaders didn't know that the Russians lacked a heat re-entry shield to protect their bombs. But we have never been a nation to shrink from a challenge. Even now, with the Russians working to give capitalism a bad name, we still can't shut up about missile defense systems. In fact, we want to build an expensive one right next door to our historically paranoid former enemy.

Anyway, Sputnik scared us so badly that Congress began demanding more weapons-grade science and math courses in our high schools. Then they gave our rehabilitated Nazi scientists carte blanche to build the kind of missiles der Führer only dreamed about, thus igniting an exorbitantly expensive race to the moon, to space shuttles and to satellites that would allow a girl to call her father in Torrance from a tiny cell phone she carried along a street in Berlin.

The Russians had the bomb, we had the bomb, we had the Strategic Air Command that routinely violated Russian airspace because we can do whatever we like. The Russians were barking mad. We didn't care.

Screw the Russians.

But not to worry. We were all protected by mutually assured destruction, which is policy-speak for it's all even-Steven. We'd set off a few bombs, they'd set off a few bombs and before you know it it's Easter. Knowing that we could kill the entire planet in 20 minutes would prevent us from doing it.

Still, to be even safer, our government did take some special precautions, my favorite being the monthly school duck-and-cover, a drill where we'd dive under our desks for a few silent moments.

Down there we'd be safe from the effects of the atomic core explosion needed to fuse deuterium with tritium and tritium with yet more tritium in an explosion equal to, say, 400,000 tons of TNT. Those temperatures, by the way, are 50 million and 400 million degrees Celsius, respectively.

Wooden desktops, meanwhile, ignite at 593 degrees Celsius while human skin begins to burn with a two-second exposure at 60 degrees Celsius.

Only we didn't know that either, which was just as well because it was terrifying enough knowing that we were safe under our desks while Mom was being vaporized like those mannequins in the Army's nuke-test films.

Those were crazy days, craziness vanquished by reason and treaty that brought the number of ready-to-go Russian and U.S. nukes down to a mere 4,000 or so.

Oh, and Thursday is also the feast day of St. Francis of Assisi, a man who celebrated life. This year I'm looking to get my dog blessed. I figure that it makes more sense than anything else I've heard in the last 50 years.

Beginning of parenthood marks the end of selfishness

October 26, 2007

"Why is my baby looking at the big, mean man?"

It so happened that I was the big, mean man in question though I was unaware of this for some oblivious minutes as I sat in an oral surgeon's waiting room reading to the sound of nurses who had emerged to coo-coo and caw over the adjacent baby and mom.

Mom, swaddled in a tent of expandable maternity clothes, had burst in moments before with grandma in tow. Sweet grandma, who bellowed at the receptionist, "I don't plan on waiting in this joint for a half-hour, honey!" Then to me, the only nonrelative in the joint, "You in here to get a tooth pulled or something?"

"No," I replied, "my son is."

"Rotten? Mine is rotten."

Not that I was about to tell her this, but his was a baby tooth hiding an impacted sideways-growing incisor that would be banded like a salmon, hooked to a tiny tow chain then attached to the braces that will pull it into place for a mere $1,500.

Tooth yanking is, of course, one of the three oldest professions. The other two are prostitution and bothering strangers in waiting rooms.

"Wait here for Grammy!" Grammy demanded before going in to lose the rotten tooth.

"Grammy is my mom," the baby's mom offered.

"She seems very nice," I lied.

"Oh, she's not," mom said, offering a hand. "I'm Trudy."

Suddenly, in one long and uninvited burst, Trudy wanted to know my son's age. She wanted to know if children become less trouble as they grow, how long it takes for them to sleep all night and do children always wreck marriages?

To this onslaught I replied: "13, no, until they reach 12 pounds and more or less."

"This is a surprise baby, a real surprise," she offered, bouncing the big-eyed creature on a knee. "I was on the pill when I got pregnant. She's 2 months old, and I've been married for seven months, get it?"

Is it just me? Or do I have the kind of face that makes people tell me things like that? Or is it a bigger issue, a systemic problem fostered by 30 years of pseudo analysis and tell-Dr.-Phil everything? Seriously this was right up there on the too-personal-scale with the day a woman in a string bikini strolled up to me at a hotel pool in Miami asking, "Do I look pregnant?"

She didn't. But here I was again, the Dutch uncle.

"I was in labor for 12 hours. Do you know what that feels like?"

No. But having been through labor a few times as an innocent bystander I can attest to pain that causes women to threaten men with both murder and divorce.

"Look, Caddie!" Trudy told the toothless baby who was smiling like a porpoise. "The man likes you!"

Caddie (I'm not making this up) is short for Cadmium, which happens to be a toxic sulfide found in zinc ore which—along with plutonium—doesn't crop up much on lists of baby names.

Trudy, it turns out, is a painter and 25, and unexpected Caddie has forced a sweet but terrible transition in her life that I told her might get written about because I write about all sorts of things.

Right about then, Trudy handed me Caddie so she could walk around the room and arch a back that has—she explained—pained her since she went from the "low hundreds to high hundreds" during pregnancy.

"I'm really a painfully thin person in a fat suit," she said, unnecessarily reminding me that women do all the heavy lifting on the road to sainted motherhood.

"You give up everything for a baby," she continued, before iterating everything that she had given up. Freedom, art, reading, walks with her boyfriend (now husband), ski weekends and the idea that she can do anything she wants.

"And I don't think any of those things are coming back," she said, looking at me like I'd have an answer when I didn't. Because all that she said was true. Babies do signal the end of some important things, but also the beginning of things far more important.

Call it sweet agony. Or just agony. But I did tell her that this was the hard part, when you're sleep-starved like a POW and ready to spill your life story on a complete stranger.

When my son appeared drugged-out and using his gauze-stuffed mouth to do a lousy Brando impression ("You come to me on this the day of my daughter's wedding and ask me to do murder."), she said, "What a beautiful boy." And she meant it like she probably couldn't have before this baby transported her to a different place.

Face it, parenthood changes us in all sorts of insane ways. For instance, I didn't even flinch when the zonked boy asked a traffic cop we came upon at a light, "What's the officer, problem?"

But it wasn't until later that I remembered what I

should have told Trudy. I should have told her that what she's feeling is the end of selfishness.

Maybe it's time to consider a reprise of that Moon House science project

January 10, 2008

I happened to mention to friend Ward Brisick that my son was rooting around for a science-fair project idea. I did this over the phone because Ward, my oldest partner in crime, lives in Australia.

How we came to be living at such a remove is probably just as remarkable as the technology that made it sound like he was calling from down the street. Down the street being where Ward lived when we met as a pair of like-minded smart-alecks in the hot summer months before seventh grade.

During our satellite-bounced conversation, Ward suggested that my son build a moon house, the Moon House being the most ill-conceived, least scientific, heaviest and—we can't explain even now—most successful science project ever produced by a pair of idiot 13-year-old boys.

The Moon House, which gets uppercase billing, may have been my idea. But it was such a singularly bad one that I'll give complete credit to Ward, who is now a successful writer and the father of two wonderfully talented children.

Alone among our smelly kid peers, we planned to capitalize on the go-go Kennedy-era space race by building a moonscape on a square of plywood. Upon this pre-moonshot fantasy would sit glass domes sheltering a lush, man-sustaining environment of the type that would no doubt be a reality by 1980.

Earth grass, earth trees and earth homes would give succor to those occupying glass bubbles connected by tubular walkways and fed by the kind of oxygen-cleansing devices that make nuclear submarine air breathable.

Our inspiration was more science fiction movie (see Zsa Zsa Gabor in "Queen of Outer Space") than science. That is to say, we did no research whatsoever. None.

But I like to think of the project as self referential. Just like Einstein's general theory of relativity, our Moon House had no precedent in all of human history. Sure, people like Arthur C. Clarke had theorized about life in space, but this was the real deal, a tangible, by-God-real Moon House taking shape in my dad's garage on a three-foot square of plywood.

The size of our platform was naturally dictated by exacting mathematical formulas, chief among them being the fact that my dad had a three-by-three scrap of plywood leaning against the lawn mower.

With this base resting on sawhorses, we began to shape our moonscape with a pound of plaster purchased at great expense from a hobby shop.

By great expense I mean $2, or about a third of a total project budget that itself amounted to most of our combined life savings. Due to some error in a plan carefully worked out using the Univac super computer (a massive machine powerful enough to work all the multiplication tables up to times-12) located at the U.S. Naval Observatory in Washington, D.C., we fell a bit short in our plaster estimation.

By short, I mean about 8-and-three-quarters of the 9 square feet total.

We immediately recalculated using a slide rule and

discovered that we wouldn't have allowance money enough to complete the project until well after we finished college. But we were enterprising lads, natural improvisers in the face of bad luck and privation. In other words, we found an open bag of cement in that same garage.

Cement, plaster, what's the difference? Besides, when mixed with water it made a lovely surface that we scalloped and cratered and had a great time with. The domes were a bit easier. We borrowed three clear Pyrex mixing bowls from my mother, who complained the entire time we had possession of them, claiming that she "used" them to prepare meals.

Under them we installed green lawns and spreading oaks bought at a model train store. There were also houses cut from squares of balsa wood and tiny people in Victorian dress because we happened to have some tiny scale model people in Victorian dress.

The domes were connected by glass rods bent over a Bunsen burner in biology class while the oxygen supply problem was solved by a set of small plastic cylinders found at the bottom of my sister's toy box and marked, "Oxygen Supply Units."

What we had on the rainy morning when Ward's mom backed her Ford Falcon station wagon up to the garage was a perfect fantasy of moon life in which people of 20 years hence dressed like people from 70 years earlier while strolling grassy laws and doing God only knows what since our domes had no air locks, gardens or waste recycling facilities.

We also had an engineering problem. You see, we were actually correct in our choice of plaster as a surface medium. I say this because we discovered too late that our three-foot-square concrete moonscape weighed the same as a three-foot-square slab of sidewalk, requiring two adults and two kids to load it and two hernias to move it from car to school library for judging.

There—and isn't this often the case with young visionaries—our science teacher (Mr. Wilmer Baird) pronounced our project a travesty. He may have even threatened to have our Moon House removed to a Dumpster so as not to cheapen real experiments on igneous rocks and the ecosystem of Florida canals and such. I say "may have" because Mr. Baird threatened Ward and me so frequently that his words tend to blur.

So it was with some surprise that a group of independent judges handed the Moon House a gold medal in the space science category.

C'mon, it took up space even if there wasn't much science in it beyond the powers of imagination. Mr. Baird, oblivious to our success, went red-faced over this. He was apoplectic, threatening, horrified, vengeful and more.

But we had the medal. Not only that, when we entered our little dodge in the county science fair competition, we won that as well. I swear it's true. And Ward will back every word that I have written.

Presidential bid adds meaning to annniversary of civil-rights massacre

February 8, 2008

My friend Sam Hammond Jr. has been on my mind lately.

Forty years ago today Sam died on the campus of South Carolina State College in Orangeburg, S.C. That night in 1968, Sam and two other young black men were killed by a fusillade of double-ought buckshot fired by S.C. state troopers to end a three-day demonstration meant to integrate a bowling alley.

The dead and most of the 27 injured, many of them coeds, were shot in the back. And this terrible violence, unfolding two years before the nation-convulsing deaths of white students at Kent State University, might never have come to light if reporter Jack Nelson hadn't written "The Orangeburg Massacre."

I last wrote about Sam a few years ago when I managed to track down Harold Riley, Sam's friend and freshman-year roommate. Riley also played on the college football team with Sam, who, after one season, was being talked about as a potential pro prospect.

Sam was that good, good-natured, caring and one of the nicest people I have ever met. He was also my first black friend, not that skin color much figured in a relationship forged in track meets and during breathless walks between practice sprints.

In a time not far removed from "colored" drinking fountains and complete segregation, when having black kids on campus was a novelty, Sam became a star in football and track. More important, he became a friend to many.

And I can't say enough about how knowing him and knowing what happened to him changed me forever.

Everything about Sam's death was surreal, starting with the way the news reached me the very next morning in my north Florida dorm room. Somehow, just that once, I was delivered a Miami Herald where—on a deep inside page—I found a photo of Sam.

Actually, it was half a picture of Sam in his Stranahan High School track sweats. I had been cropped out but I could see my arm around Sam's shoulder and recall how excited we were to have that photo taken on top of just being excited to be 17, fast and alive.

Sam had been killed in what the wire service story called a "race riot." Sam in a race riot? It didn't figure and I said so in a letter that I wrote to my hometown paper, the Fort Lauderdale News/Sun Sentinel. A few years later, Nelson included that heartbroken piece in his book. It would later find its way into social studies texts with its utterly powerless final line, "I feel that someone has killed my brother."

Nelson would also reveal an FBI cover-up and a complete lack of public concern over an event, the brutality of which was summed up by Harold Riley—now retired and living in Greensboro, N.C.—who recalls state troopers dragging two mortally wounded black teens down an embankment by the feet with one of them scolding, "None of this would have happened if you niggers had stayed home where you belong."

I wouldn't have been surprised in the least to hear

such a thing in the South of that bygone time, in a place where cruelty was casually meted out, cruelty that left Sam and me eating alone on the bus off paper plates during track road trips because diners wouldn't serve him.

But it wasn't until I spoke to Riley that I found out how right I was. Sam had wandered into the killing zone after dinner that night just to see what was going on.

"Sam went on down the line. Then came the whistle. I'll never forget that. Then the shooting, eight or 10 seconds of steady shotgun fire like it was planned because it ended with a second whistle," Riley recalled about the evening he took bullet fragments that still remain lodged in his knees.

The hardest part is knowing that there were no ambulances called and only a single nurse in the student infirmary to send the wounded and dying to hospitals in commandeered cars.

Said Riley, "I saw Sam there on the infirmary floor, nobody tending him. He was staring straight up, glassy-eyed, mumbling. We were just in there hurt and scared with no security, no doctors, nobody on our side."

With nobody at his side, my friend Sam died at 11:30 p.m. on February 8, 1968, calling out for the mother that he would never see again.

In time the only person convicted of anything was a young black student organizer. A federal inquest later exonerated the shooters, believing that they had fired in self-defense on what is overwhelmingly believed to be unarmed teens. Even black leaders ignored the killings.

Still Sam's name is rightly engraved on the Civil Rights Memorial in Montgomery, Ala., along with 39 other men, women and children. Martyrs all. The last name cut into the black stone was the Rev. Martin Luther King Jr., who would join Sam in death less than two months later.

Which makes this a sad and terrible anniversary year

in an America now much changed, an America that has gone from black and white to black, white and absolutely everyone else. But most remarkable to those of us with long memories is how, in this changed nation, a black man can run for the presidency, being loved by many and reviled by some not for the color of his skin but for his politics.

It's this better-seeming America that I wish Sam could have seen, an America where he might have done all the usual things, where he might have fallen in love, married and had children that couldn't be forced by anybody to eat alone on a bus, an America that would have just allowed him to live.

'Somewhere else' cousin lives on in memory

April 25, 2008

My cousin Frankie died last week, which isn't any more newsworthy than the death of any other cousin anywhere except for what his passing says about life and how we perceive our place in its tumultuous flow.

Frankie was the oldest of all the cousins, an adult from the start. Maybe he was born older, like George Bailey, or maybe it was just the way little kids see older kids. Which is to say, infinitely more mature and already inscrutable in the way of grown-ups—funny rarely, serious often and always with things that needed doing and places that needed going.

Frankie was a product of my mother's second sister, Polly. Her real name was Columbia, which was meant to be a tribute to both Columbus and this great land that her parents took a big chance on. These were people who came here with hope in their hearts and no expectation that they would do anything but work ceaselessly and bring their four daughters early to the factory floor.

So they all toiled and they all prospered in the usual way. And all four daughters had children, 12 to be exact, and I am the second to the youngest. Frankie was the oldest, 15 years my senior and always it seemed somewhere else with his girlfriend, Helen.

Helen of the bubbly voice, red hair and great smile. She was the exact opposite of Frankie, who had the stern face of a southern Italian. Like his dad, Frankie Sr., he was a carpenter and I recall being greatly impressed by the way he could nail down studs with nobody yelling at him because he did something wrong.

While Frankie ruled wood-fragrant construction sites, I was still being wised-up by adults who criticized mercilessly. Which is why I say that my children are like I might have been had I not spent the first 15 years of my life hearing, "What the hell's the matter with you?"

Still, I had it pretty good in an America just then developing bigger expectations than the ones experienced by our parents. College was being talked about for the first time in our family along with new cars and better houses. It sounds like all the usual now. But there was a time when it was anything but.

In fact, one of the first signs of our family's growing prosperity was Frankie's car, a huge blue Ford that he drove to his own wedding in a church that resembled a birthday cake on acid.

Afterward, after the kids all had their faces pinched by old women who resembled Cossacks, we had a typical reception at the Sons of Italy with the entire family taking part in what was essentially a food-preparation religion with the pasta, veal and the cellar-wine decanted into gallon glass jugs and sealed with wax paper and rubber bands.

After that, Frankie and Helen moved into the apartment we owned on the top floor of our house, which I mention because what happened next was typical of our batty extended family.

Frankie came in under an agreement that he'd paint the place for a cut in rent. And sure enough, he painted and painted and it was kind of nice having him around to start renovation projects for my mother that he'd never finish.

When he moved out a couple of years later, we found that Frankie had painted without bothering to move the furniture or pictures. Which made the joint look like it had been targeted by some sort of advanced thermal bomb that had taken out everything and left behind on the walls only furniture and picture shadows.

My mother was furious but she couldn't say anything because Frankie was her sister's son. Only the story got told to absolutely everyone else while I wound up painting out the shadows of Frankie's domestic life that would soon include a divorce from beautiful Helen.

So I'm left to deal with memory bits. Why, for instance, would I still be carrying around an argument we had over Jerry Lewis. Frankie was a huge fan of the serious, bawling, telethon Jerry while I absolutely loved (c'mon, I was 9) slapstick, "Pretty lady!" Jerry.

I even remember the argument because it was the first I ever won against an adult. Frankie said something about how he liked the comic best when he wasn't being a comic and I said that a comic not being funny was a waste of time, adding, "And what kind of idiot paints around furniture?" That's when he tried to smack me. Which was when I knew that I had won.

After that, things went south, literally. The entire family moved to Florida. Frankie stayed behind, remarrying and having children, second cousins that I've never met.

I don't even know their names, which is indicative of what happened when the grandparents died, taking with them the glue that bound us.

I'd hear about Frankie. He did things for charity. He made custom doghouses. He did OK for himself but I never again saw him because I had become what he had once been, the kid who was always somewhere else.

Then he died. Like a book that I always meant to read, he became forever unreadable, passing beyond everything but faulty memory. And the significance of this is obvious to anyone living within the mortal batting order of siblings and cousins.

Frankie was the first of our first generation to plop into this American life. And he is the first to vanish.

I'm aware that we don't all leave in the order that we arrived. Life offers no ensured chronology. Still, who would want it any other way than first in, first out, top to bottom? So, we've all gotten our unspoken wish to this sad extent. Frankie died first, the oldest, the eternal adult who inexplicably liked serious Jerry. He's gone and who's next is who's next.

Love isn't always as simple as black and white

May 13, 2008

I remember the story because of what the grown-ups said. They said that it would set a bad example and cause a decline in morality, they said giving those people an inch of freedom would only make them want a mile, they said that it was just wrong and against the Bible's teachings.

They asked, the grown-ups did, "Could you imagine going to bed with a woman like that?" They wondered aloud, "What would their poor children look like?" Most important, they asked, "Where would they expect to live?" Then they answered their own question, "Not around here, that's for sure!"

Then I saw a photograph in the newspaper of this bad example, this terrible and awful thing. And though I was still a child, I was wising up fast and realizing that the grown-ups were not always right. In fact, they were often laughably off base, especially in this instance because the news photos making the grown-ups shake their wise heads and curse was just a picture of two other grown-ups—Mildred and Richard Loving.

And I thought that that was a grand name, Loving. It was like the husband in "Lady and the Tramp" being called "Jim, dear" by his wife. I figured if I ever managed to grow up, I'd want a woman to call me "dear" with such sweet familiarity.

And I'd want that to happen in a country where people like the Lovings could do what they wanted, what they had already done by the hot July in 1958 when Caroline County, Va., sheriff's deputies broke in at 2 a.m. and surrounded the bed of the young newlyweds demanding to know which of them was Mildred Loving.

That should have been obvious to the crackers, but the law is the law. And the law in Virginia since 1691—with bumps from laws passed in 1878 and one approved in 1924 called the Racial Integrity Act—made it a felony punishable by up to five years in prison for black people and white people to marry.

God forbid.

In fact, that 1878 law even made it illegal for mixed-race couples like the Lovings—she was black, he was white—to marry elsewhere and return to Virginia, which is what they did.

And it wasn't just Virginia or even just the Deep South. At that time, half the states in the Land of The Free did not allow mixed-race marriages. The law prohibiting such dreadful genetic mixing put us in harmonious line with other virulent anti-miscegenation regimes, most notably South Africa and the then-not-so-long-departed Nazi Third Reich.

Purity is purity and white is right. And if it isn't, the least we can do is feed the silly myth.

Or so the thinking, or non-thinking, went.

For Mildred Loving—a soft-spoken, kind-faced country-raised woman who always hated the spotlight—the issue seemed simple enough. In 1967 she told ABC News, "I think marrying who you want is a right no man should have anything to do with. It's a God-given right."

Well, I never!

Indicted under that 1924 law, the Lovings pleaded guilty to, well, loving each other and to committing the nation-destroying crime of marriage. They couldn't very well deny it.

A judge sentenced them to a year in jail and then suspended the sentence for 25 years on condition that the couple leave the state and not return as long as they remained married.

I didn't know that such a thing could happen in America, but they were—this dues-paying American couple—literally exiled to Washington, D.C., with no hope short of divorce for returning.

By 1963, homesick and missing their families, they appealed to Attorney General Robert Kennedy, who referred the case to the ACLU, which brought it before the Supreme Court in 1967. There, in a 9-0 vote, the justices ruled that this last-to-fall white supremacy law violated the 14th Amendment. That's the pesky due process and equal protection rule that is so easily ignored by people who can't read.

Things have, of course, changed vastly since 1967, with the most obvious of those changes being how we have gone from a white/black country to a land of all races.

Interracial marriages, which are narrowly defined by the U.S. Census Bureau as either white/black or white/Asian, numbered 310,000 in 1970. By 1980 that figure had risen to 651,000. By 2000 the number was 2,669,558, or 4.9 percent of all marriages.

What's more, the grown-ups were dead wrong. The nation didn't fall apart, people didn't go on to marry cattle and horses, and whatever bad stuff was supposed to happen because of this never happened. And if bad-stuff did happen, it wasn't generally because of people falling in love.

Richard Loving was killed by a drunken driver in

1975. Mildred Loving—mother of two, grandmother to eight and great-grandmother to 11—died just last week of pneumonia at age 70. She was one month short of what would have been her 50th wedding anniversary.

She never remarried.

Which brings me to another couple—one black, one white, professional women both and partners for 30 years who can't legally marry.

What do the grown-ups say about them?

Finding room for Holy Spirit at grad time

June 2, 2008

I didn't get an eighth-grade graduation. In fact, the only acknowledgment of this non-event came with my dad sniffing, "That was the year I dropped out and joined the Navy."

I bring this up because eighth-grade graduation, at my son's Catholic school anyway, has grown into a very big deal. Actually, it's a preposterously big deal. And I mean nothing even remotely critical when I say that the good women who elevated this once low-key ceremony into a gala celebration are people with far too much time on their hands.

Somehow, mothers at this school have gone—during our rewarding 18-year association with the place—from women who work to women (educated, smart, talented and good looking) who assemble yearbooks, take class pictures, order caps and gowns and organize graduation activities that I couldn't have dreamed up with the help of six double vodka martinis.

Which is just an exaggeration. But we all know that vodka is a gateway drug that leads to all sorts of strange behaviors. Behaviors that might indeed include a graduation church service followed by a graduation breakfast with awards, followed on the same evening by yet another graduation service followed by yet another presentation of awards, followed by the first of two dances.

Naturally, part of the blame falls to AYSO, the otherwise fantastic soccer organization that introduced into an America once defined by cut-throat Little League competition and bellowing Pop Warner coaches a system whereby everybody is important enough to get an award even if they habitually leave the field midplay to take a break on dad's lap.

In keeping with this everybody's-a-star tradition, the 30 students in my son's class received a combined total of 15,787 awards. So many awards handed out—with nobody telling the assembled parents, grandparents, aunts, uncles, siblings and cousins to hold their aching applause—I was certain that they'd award each graduate one of those white plastic Postal Service boxes to carry the things.

There were academic awards and awards from the high schools where the students were heading, there were athletic awards for all the sports; student council awards; altar server awards; choir awards; class leadership awards; awards for participating in the great books, chess, drama, writing, journalism, Latin, French and dance clubs; awards from adult service clubs that came with scholarship money; awards from the company that engraved the awards and, I don't know, best smile awards.

Of course, there were no awards for the 60 million parent/teacher hours it took to get them all here because that reward comes in heaven.

Then my son got a presidential award for academic achievement. Not to dull the significance of a beautifully embossed certificate "signed" by someone claiming to be President Bush, but my kid has a 3.3 GPA. Which, in an age of ever-upward GPA-creep, isn't anything that would stand out anywhere but on any NCAA sports team.

Still, it was nice of GW to think of the boy, who also received an award that I never heard of because it didn't exist when his older sisters graduated. Called the Pastor's Award, it is voted on by the class and presented, along with 300 smackers, to the best all-around student. This I mention only because of what would transpire the following evening.

Then it was off to a post-graduation dinner dance meant to cap the long day that the tassled kids seemed to enjoy immensely. This turned out to be a supervised rave with the 30 graduates and an army of high-energy younger siblings going absolutely bonkers on a dance floor.

Naturally, I sat next to somebody's Uncle Morty, who was hard of hearing and couldn't quite understand what I was saying. I figured this out when, over the din, he introduced me as a "communist" to his brother Louie.

"Great, a red!" Louie shouted.

But the best thing was the next night's final dance, the one staged in the church hall with a Hollywood theme, with dads on the door and the moms hunkered in the kitchen with wine for themselves and massive amounts of food for the ravenous kids who—after being together nearly every day since age 5—still find one another endlessly interesting.

This seemed especially true of the boys who, dressed in suits bought just a little big so they could grow into them, were not used to seeing their female classmates in something other than a wool and sackcloth Catholic school uniforms.

And it is still true, even with all the advances in acne medication, that girls of that age look like young women while the boys still look like hopeless geeks. Still, the entire fog-machine-and-tinsel evening got off to a start that I recognized immediately because I once lived it.

As the girls danced with each other, the boys formed into a kind of black-suited scrum with the tall alpha boys at the center and the shorter boys on the perimeter.

Eventually they'd start dancing, tall boys with short girls and short boys with very tall girls, and it looked at first so painful that I decided not to haunt the dance floor with a flashlight—as tiny Sister Mary Immaculata did in my youth—warning them all to leave room for the Holy Spirit.

Finally, in all that fake fog and DJ din, the girls started crying over the realization that this society, this extended accidental family that they had taken as permanent and forever, was about to fracture. The boys, big-hearted and kind, immediately grasped this moment of female weakness to offer embraces that left no room at all for the Holy Spirit.

At one point, my son came over to thank the parental kitchen staff that had, by the way, completely ignored the no-drinking order instituted by the school's principal. The kid was fantastic, a regular Eddie Haskel thanking every drunk in the room.

Then, grinning and winking, Pastor's-Award-boy whispered, "Excuse me, the girls need more comforting."

Fraternity mom evokes way women were

July 13, 2008

Mom Ruth Woods died last week in Atlanta. She was 92 years old and, for 15 years back during the 1960s and 1970s, this sedate woman was housemother to my fraternity at the University of Florida.

She also had the maybe not-so-unusual distinction of disliking me intensely. I'd use the word "hate," but Mom Woods was too well-mannered to express such an emotion except in the most delicate of ways.

An example of this delicacy being how she once turned to the chapter president sitting beside her at dinner demanding—while looking directly at me as I waited tables in exchange for food—"Tell that buffoon to take that hat off!"

The hat in question—this final straw—was a borrowed off-white Stetson 10-gallon and it helps provide here the tiniest glimpse into that nearly vanished corner of American "civilization."

I'm talking here about the late 1960s. America was unraveling like a cheap suit while our fraternity sauntered blissfully along in the still unabashedly segregated Deep South.

First you have to know something about me at age

18. I was a jerk—you're not surprised?—a noisy, full-on Northern boy exiled to north-central Florida, to a time warp of fraternity pins and Sigma Chi sweethearts.

Seriously, even as we pledges were forced to serenade before Spanish-moss-hung, neoclassical sorority houses—even as I tried to fit in—I'd be the one looked upon by the stiff-haired maidens within like I was wearing Slinky-eyed novelty glasses.

I'd compare that bygone era to "Animal House," and that would be accurate description if most of the fraternities on campus at that time weren't like the straight house next door to the one where John Belushi lived. Sure, there were houses that I might have fit into better, but the Jewish kids wouldn't have me.

And I had but one reason to enter into this throwback society where I clearly did not belong. I didn't want to be a dorm geek, you know, a freshmen who didn't fit into cool-guy Greek life. Which pretty much tells you everything that we need to know about doing the wrong thing for the wrong reason.

A day would soon arrive when I would find my own way on that sprawling campus. But for that year I was stuck in its gooey amber as part of what may still be the only Sigma Chi pledge class ever held back a semester for initiation.

You see, there were others like me in that class, full-of-hell guys with bad attitudes bridling at the strange things fraternities then required of freshmen who were having a hard enough time just staying in school.

As a pledge, being forced to learn the names of all the brothers was one thing. But knowing their names, majors and hometowns was quite another, especially when there were more than 100 of them.

But the most galling requirement was that we memorize the name, hometown and major of every Villager-dress-wearing bubblehead that our elders had given their fraternity pins to as down payment on the drunken dream wedding to follow, the big ceremony that would open the golden door on the kind of life that I would have opened an artery to avoid.

Actually, it was the kind of life—full of family, dogs and unkempt lawns—that I would take up belatedly and with great joy.

Only right then I was chafing at all things represented by this organization that I joined of my own free will. Joining up with guys who expected me to take seriously a dress code (down to wearing socks and hard shoes) and worse, guys who frowned upon the women that I dated, women who definitely weren't going to make the sweetheart court. But they certainly were my sweethearts all the way down to their sweetly bare hippie feet.

In some ways, I felt like the only person in the place who was still 18. Naturally, I was wrong as I am about so many things. Still, this was an organization of men who spoke of the manly things that I was determined to avoid.

Suspended in this mix was Mom Woods. Mom lived in an apartment attached to the house, a cool, carpeted, civilized place full of delicate figurines and ticking mantle clocks. And while I never knew what the gig paid, I did know that it included room, meals and no real job description.

But I figured that the main reason she was there, the main reason such women were part of every house on campus, was to keep order. Not by force and not in the masculine way, which would have meant a lot of yelling.

No, all Mom had to do was show up all serene in pearls and sweater looking like Nancy Reagan and all the other women of her generation who put ladylike behavior ahead of all things. She was, in short, a member of the last American generation to do so, the last generation we can point to and ask, "Remember when women behaved in just that way?"

I guess that I would have liked to have Mom Woods as a friend because I was also truly lost in those days, cut off from the people who loved me and stranded in a cold and indifferent place that clearly did not.

Naturally, my antics offended her. Soon I was invisible. I wasn't looked at or spoken to, she didn't sew buttons on my shirts or offer me cookies and cocoa like she did the other guys. Mom was, in her dignified way, proof of my mistake.

A mistake that still, for all my complaining, brought me friends that I have until this day. Friends like Phil Combest who e-mailed me the news of Mom's death the other day from Miami.

So, you see, she was a much-loved mom to many, but not me. And she was respected by many, me included, for maintaining standards that did not include something as idiotic as wearing a cowboy hat at dinner and for always knowing, while never betraying, exactly who she was.

Love and family at the heart of the matter

July 17, 2008

The technician working the echocardiogram had more important things to do than deal with the worried dad leaning over her shoulder.

"That's the mitral valve, isn't it?" I asked. "His mother has a mitral valve defect so I know that one."

"That's the aortic valve," she corrected as vivid reds and blues shot through the heart that was, at that moment, keeping my casually reclining son alive enough to watch "Shrek" on a flat-screen monitor.

"The kid has a Scottish gene pool rotten with leaky mitral valves," I added. "The hearts on his Italian side were good, only eveybody was crazy."

"Maybe you'd be more comfortable in the hall," replied the technician."

"Don't make him wait in the hall," my son protested. "He'll just bother everyone out there."

If there is a pattern in my life it is this: I ask too many questions. This is never more true than when the health of my children, or the health of children in general, comes into question. Then I'm a parrot on meth.

Look, I know how I'm supposed to be. I'm supposed to be cool and dispassionate. Only I can't be, not when I'm sitting in a cardiologist's waiting room with a possibly sick son, a dozen possibly sick or actively sick babies and their worried-sick parents.

Maybe I was more worried for the parents because I know what it takes to bring a child into the world and I know the willingness to give a kid your own beating heart just because he needs a shot and because kids are the surest sign that the divine wants our sorry race to survive.

Of course, we were there for nothing. That's what our pediatrician said, "It's nothing." With the "nothing" in question being chest pains. But wait, if it's nothing, why are we going to see a pediatric cardiologist, one of those subset specialties that in my mind spells big trouble and trips to important hospitals in far-off cities?

"We just want to be sure," his doctor said.

"Sure of what?" I began.

"Sure of anything that might be wrong, but I'm sure it's nothing."

"Then why are we going?" I asked, sounding exactly like all my crazy ancestors and relatives.

So we were dealing with nothing, one father and one son who looked like he didn't have a care in the world because, as he put it, "Worrying is your job."

By the way, if you are contemplating parenthood, consider the boy's words, consider our presence in a pediatric cardiologist's office and keep in mind that this sort of thing never really ends even when they are all grown up and calling from New York City because they can't remember which museum has the mounted-knight exhibit.

It's the Metropolitan.

We began with a quite normal EKG. Then the doctor, a real New York smart guy with a good manner, listened to his chest, prodding, poking and taking blood pressure before pronouncing him likely to outlive everyone in that room. Which wasn't saying much since the doctor and I were the same age.

Next came the echocardiogram, which is much like the long-ago sonogram that told me a boy—rather than the expected third girl—was on his way.

Here's what I told the pediatrician way back then: "It can't be a boy, we only have girls." This is what the pediatrician told me while pointing to the monitor: "See that? That's not his thumb."

And so it wasn't. Now here we were again. Only this time an even better machine was deconstructing the boy's heart, turning it upside down and viewing it from every possible angle as it hammered and pumped in its dazzling and mysterious way.

I suddenly remembered asking a junior high biology teacher why hearts beat.

"Why? You're asking for the secret of life. I don't know that," he replied.

Actually, I got a more-how-than-why answer from the Texas Heart Institute information center Web site, which explains that electrical impulses from the heart muscle (the myocardium) cause the heart to contract. This electrical signal begins in the sinoatrial node which is the heart's pacemaker. This electrical impulse travels through the muscle fibers of the atria and ventricles, causing them to contract.

And there it was, 7 to 15 ounces of miracle beating away in my son's chest. During an average human life a heart beats 3.5 billion times. That's 100,000 beats pushing 2,000 gallons of blood through 60,000 miles of blood vessels each live-long day.

Certainly my father never studied anything about me much less my precious pericardium, which is the double-layered membrane (and engineering marvel) surrounding the heart. The outer layer of the pericardium surrounds the roots of the heart's major blood vessels and is attached by ligaments to the spinal column, diaphragm and other handy body parts.

Are you following this?

Meanwhile, the inner layer is attached to the heart muscle with a coating of fluid separating the two layers. This is what allows the heart to move about as it beats, allows it to stay attached through childbirth, 100-meter dashes, sex and presidential speeches.

And it works like a Swiss watch, this collection of left and right atria, left and right ventricles and the four valves—the tricuspid, pulmonary, aortic and mitral. The mitral, the boy's hereditary concern, lets oxygen-rich blood from his lungs pass from the left atrium into his much-loved left ventricle.

Only his was fine.

"Perfect," the doctor said, adding that the pains could be this or that and not to worry. "Now, do you need something to calm down?"

This he asked me.

And yes, yes I did.

But no, no I wouldn't because the boy is fine. He's also a miracle bound up in a great and truly wondrous why.

Death may not be proud, but it is honest

August 19, 2008

As obituaries go, this one from the Vallejo Times-Herald sets a standard for brutal honesty. It also brings to mind this idea that all stories are about love or the lack of love.

"Dolores Aguilar, born in 1929 in New Mexico, left us on August 7, 2008. Dolores had no hobbies, made no contribution to society and rarely shared a kind word or deed in her life. I speak for the majority of her family when I say her presence will not be missed by many, very few tears will be shed and there will be no lamenting over her passing.

"Her family will remember Dolores and amongst ourselves we will remember her in our own way, which were mostly sad and troubling times throughout the years. We may have some fond memories of her and perhaps we will think of those times, too. But I truly believe at the end of the day all of us will really only miss what we never had, a good and kind mother, grandmother and great-grandmother. I hope she is finally at peace with herself. As for the rest of us left behind, I hope this is the beginning of a time of healing and learning to be a family again.

"There will be no service, no prayers and no closure for the family she spent a lifetime tearing apart. We cannot come together in the end to see to it that her grandchildren and great-grandchildren can say their goodbyes. So I say here for all of us, goodbye Mom."

This was strange enough to make me check Snopes.com, a dispeller of e-myth, before calling the Vallejo Times-Herald and speaking to Editor Ted Vollmer, who said that the paid obit that ran in his paper Friday and Saturday was indeed real.

"We even requested a copy of the death certificate, something we rarely do, to make sure that it wasn't a scam," said Vollmer, who then gave me the phone number of Virginia Brown, a Seattle resident and the woman who wrote the obituary that is now rocketing around cyberspace.

I caught up with Brown, one of Aguilar's eight children, at work on Monday morning.

"I wanted to do the right thing, the honest thing," said the 54-year-old mother of two. "When she died a co-worker gave me a copy of an obituary she wrote for her father as a kind of writing guide. What struck me was how my mother was none of the things I was reading. She was never there for us, she was never good and she left no legacy. So how could I say any of the usual things about her?"

What you see above is a distillation of eight first-draft pages crammed with the sad story of a woman who, Brown said, probably suffered from never-diagnosed mental disorders that caused her to keep her children unfed, poorly clothed and completely terrorized.

"She was a chameleon. She could make outsiders see her in any way that she wanted while behind closed doors she would beat at least one of us every day," Brown said of her San Francisco childhood. "She left all of us struggling. We just never learned how to cope with life.

Our father, meanwhile, was a good man. My only hope for him was that he would outlive her just long enough to know some happiness. Only he didn't."

These bitter memories have kept the many siblings apart. Seeing each other, she said, only dredges up a common past that they all want to forget.

Brown wrote the piece alone but has yet to hear any disagreement from the family members who have seen it in the three days since it ran in her mother's hometown. Nor has the paper received any.

"I wrote the truth," Brown insisted, throwing harsh light on a portion of the death business that routinely has loved ones being borne away to that "better place."

But don't think that I am making light of a reality that we attempt to contain with such benign images. Though a more measured story of lives lived and ended might prove more enriching for those left behind.

As a child, I read newspaper obits for direction, searching for stories of men who did fantastic and selfless things to save others.

I still read the obituaries even though they now come in two forms, the famous-person obit and the paid, formulaic obit like the one stood on its head by Brown.

End-stories of the famous are generally written in advance and maintained in go-condition by big news organizations. These short-form tell-alls fold failures and successes into stories that often tell us everything we need to know about the passing nature of glory.

But ever since newspapers went to paid obituaries we have been deprived of the smaller views of everyday lives. These days it's the "Beloved father of ... passed away on ... veteran of ... member of ... he loved life ... survived by ... " And rarely do we even read the cause of death let alone some telling detail of the good fight.

Occasionally someone will stretch the form to tell us in bought space that, "If there is a heaven, Bob is now hoisting one with God."

Often, when a death becomes news, we run into the usual contradictions. A former gang member shot to death had given up gangs. A felon shot by police had very nearly gotten his life together.

It would seem that there is little need among the living to tarnish even the most wasted lives.

Which is what makes Brown's writing so unusual, so seemingly brutal and so hard to take in a world where we just as soon let our dead depart for that better place without an honest word to inform us or even make us feel.

High school, Dockers an uneasy fit

August 26, 2008

Buying trousers for a 14-year-old boy is not easy. This is especially true when the boy is tall, when he is all thin arms and long legs, when he is all hands, feet and banjo eyes.

And hair.

Though the hair doesn't figure into the trouser equation, it does figure into mornings, noons and a period just post-shower when I might find the Boy Wonder in front of a bathroom mirror with thick hair slicked back doing a bad Michael Corleone impression, "After the baptism I take care of Stracci, Cuneo, Tattaglia, Barzini, all the heads of the five families."

Oh, and skin. Like someone exposed to chemical warfare, his skin has become an often-cleansed, ointment-slathered indicator of the hormone rage within.

I'm convinced that this violent change from child to young man is the real-life template for the werewolf legend. If you want to see a human body going wretchedly from one thing to another thing entirely, going from sweetness and light to something unrecognizable and alien, look no further.

Sure, I'm a sap when it comes to kids and I am being a bigger sap than usual just now as my last child enters high school, as he makes the move from middle school to the full-on terror-scape of permanent records, SATs, college acceptance and daily life fraught with upperclassmen who look old enough to be somebody's father. And might be.

It was either Yogi Berra or educational philosopher Jean Piaget who said that this is the most disappointing developmental stage for parents, this moment when our children stop being cute and start being endearing werewolves.

Piaget, father of the "constructivist theory of knowing," also observed "that it is impossible to buy 14-year-old boys decent-fitting pants."

So maybe he didn't actually say that. But he might have had he gone hunting beige Dockers in stores that no longer carry tape measures, stores staffed by too-few sales clerks who (seriously) don't even know what a tape measure is.

This in places already sacked by parents who, like me, have a kid going to a high school that requires the aforementioned Dockers. A school that naturally assumes that a dad assigned the task of boy-shopping would not wait until the very last minute to visit a department store where a clerk might say, "The moms cleaned out the Dockers weeks ago."

That's the key, moms who know how to shop and dads who wait until it's too late. And, yes, bright people, I do know that Dockers—like nuclear bomb triggers and Aeroflot tickets—are available online.

Only not when you're dealing with a slouching, slab-stomached creation that was somehow born without hips, with a boy who can try on two items of same-brand, same-size clothing and have one fit and the other not.

Worse, like most boys, he has no interest in trying on anything without the name of a skateboard maker printed on it because, as he asked, "What does it really matter?"

So it was time for boy philosopher to learn that the existence of existentialism does not excuse us from paying taxes or buying the required Dockers.

But doing this required the kind of older-father guile that you younger dads will one day develop if you are completely unlucky. What we did was visit a Macy's well out of the general area of his high school. It was there, 30 minutes distant, that we destroyed the Docker display by trying on 20 pairs of beige pants, finally finding three that actually fit.

Wait, maybe "fit" is too grand a word. With a 28-inch "waist" and a 31-inch length, they barely stayed up, even with the help of a required leather belt that he didn't want either. But he was ready, finally, outfitted with several solid-colored polo shirts and spanking-new sneakers.

Actually, "ready" isn't the right word either. He had jitters, jitters no different than those experienced by his older sisters at his age, only he had his quietly. And it didn't matter that they both told him chin-up and don't worry. Naturally enough, he was worried about the things young boys have worried about since our early days hunting on the plains of Africa.

If all his concerns could be boiled down, they would boil down to this. What if I don't make it?

I, of course, knew that he would because he's a good kid and a funny kid with great hair and new clothing that we washed three times so they wouldn't look so glaringly freshman-like.

Then there was this other thing. Ever since he was a little guy, boy wonder would always tell me that he loved me when we parted ways. And he didn't much care who heard him. Now, on the way to his very first morning of high school, he said, "We need a code. Instead of telling you that I love you, I'll just say, 'Later, Dad.' You'll know what I mean."

The code seemed much more reasonable in the school's drop-off lane, where older boys were leaving cars carrying shoulder pads and walking with the heavy, bandaged gravitas of gladiators that could spot fresh meat at 20 paces no matter how many times a mom washed the Dockers.

"These guys are the size of lowland gorillas," he said, gawping at the passing parade of lowland gorillas. He drew a deep breath, "Well, this is it."

Then he touched my hand, "Later, Dad."

Later, son.

Old-line editor knew the magic of words

December 5, 2008

You didn't know him, not directly anyway. His name was Fred Pettijohn and he died on October 1 in Florida at age 91. During my childhood he was editor of the Fort Lauderdale News and Sun-Sentinel and the father of a good friend.

He was also a truth guardian in the old sense and a fabulous role model. Which is to say that I wanted to be exactly like him. More accurately, I wanted to be what he was, smart. Not smart like a lawyer but smart like a newspaperman, a label that is now nearly meaningless.

Newspapers were bigger in Pettijohn's time and singularly important. In fact, our then smallish south Florida town had these two publications and heavy competition from a local bureau of the Miami Herald.

But newspaper reporters and editors were even then a rare and quirky human commodity. Cerebral and profane, these old-time wise guys seemed to run on coffee and cigarettes in a business that I'd find a small place in when I was still in high school. Which is to say that I'd go in weekends to file sports photographs and, from time to time, be allowed to cover a football or baseball game if the stakes were low enough.

Mainly what I did was watch the reporters in their filthy, clamorous newsroom, in a time of typewriters, carbon paper and inky page proofs, in a time of secreted booze and loud talk. It was a wretched, doughnut-crumbed, drink-spilled, disgusting place and I loved it instantly.

Most of all I admired Pettijohn, a slender, almost professorial man in black-rimmed glasses and starched shirts, a man exuding intellect and cool confidence who would each day take a seat in a tiny sound-proof booth to deliver radio commentaries that began, "Hi, friends."

I'd sometimes spot him through the glass wall of the sports department and wonder at his effortless grasp of two mediums that began with the magical placement of words on paper.

I'd see him off-duty as well, mainly in the big sun room of his splendid old house on the New River. In that cool, awning-shaded place he would read with a keen intensity that I had then only seen in him. Years later I'd understand that he was parsing each sentence and paragraph as writers do, getting to the heart of how it was assembled, how it lived and breathed and took its place on a page.

Much later a friend, Ward Brisick, and I started an underground newspaper in our college town. Like me, Ward had grown up around this man, so naturally he took him a copy of our small effort as a kind of offering. Pettijohn offered comments and advice, Ward reminded me the other day from his home in Australia, and was "gracious as always." Then he surprised him by asking, "I hear that you have Kenny 'The Cat' Boyden working for you?"

Our hippie paper did indeed have Boyden filling our news racks as part of his work-release from Raiford State Penitentiary. Only we didn't know that Kenny, once a partner of the infamous Murf "The Surf" Murphy, had in 1964 allegedly been in on stealing the 563-carat Star of India sapphire from Manhattan's Museum of Natural History. The point here being that Pettijohn was always plugged in.

He retired years ago and when I last spoke to his son, Phil, in Tallahassee, I asked him to tell his father that his example had helped shape my life. Phil said that he probably wouldn't relay my thanks because a lot of old reporters say the same thing and he just wouldn't accept credit or praise.

Recently an old colleague of Pettijohn's, John de Groot, offered the following tribute on the Sun-Sentinel Web site in the form of a commentary written by the late editor for the first edition of the paper on April 11, 1960.

"This is the way a newspaper is born ... ," he wrote of his new publication in an ellipses-rife style. "It comes onto the world without any yesterdays ... only tomorrows ... the more tomorrows the better. Conceived by need, carried in confusion, it's birthed only by labor and the strange love that men in this business have for the printed page. Its veins run with printers ink and the commodity it breathes goes on ... and grows on, is just one thing ... the news.

"You don't spank a baby newspaper's bottom to make it cry ... you expect it in its first day of life to show maturity ... Yes, and strength and character, too. For without these, no baby newspaper survives. The food of the newspaper is its readership, its content, the needs it fulfills ... and the vital factors of depth, perception and decency. For the wisest parents, ask only that their child grow into a decent human being. And that is all important with infant newspapers, too.

"Few businesses or professions ask more of their employees than a newspaper. Labor necessitates that a man work with his hands. The crafts ask that a man work with his head. The art field needs a man who works with his heart. And sales require a man to work with his feet. A newspaper demands that a man work with all four. That is because a newspaper ... must be a register of the times ... a daily account of living history, a faithful reporter of every species of intelligence.

"A newspaper ought not to be engrossed by any one particular object but, like a well-planned meal, it should contain something suited to every taste, to every need. To accomplish this requires not only a touch of inspiration, but also close study and constant attention to the public and its interests ...

"If I have perhaps burdened you with our professional problems, forgive me. I felt it was something you would want to know because, you see, this (new publication) is not just our baby, it is yours, too. And we hope you'll be happy to have it in your life."

But not as happy and honored as I was, even tangentially, to have him in mine.

Long-loved voice silent, but still heard

March 2, 2009

If we are lucky, and I was, someone like Helen Hanrahan Cola will shape our lives.

Helen was a rare person, the first person to treat me like an adult, the first adult to value my opinions, the person who explained modernism to me, who showered me with attention and later—during a destitute moment—welcomed me in off the street.

I met Helen—Hanni I called her—just after meeting her son, David, in seventh grade. She couldn't have been far into her 30s at that time in the early 1960s, when being a divorced mother of three young sons was rare enough.

Being a divorced, college-educated mother with a career as a newspaper photographer put her so far ahead of her time she was out of time, operating in a dimension all her own.

To me and so many other boys my age, she was like

something from a far better world, a slender Jackie Kennedy type who spoke foreign languages and traveled far on jets.

She was also my dream mom, the one person who saw in me and so many other strays brought in by her gregarious and intelligent sons all the things that we couldn't. There was vast generosity in her coupled with cool. Her book-filled house, with the real art and the expensive camera equipment mixed with the unfolded laundry, was an island of enlightenment in a sea of conformity.

Some may have preferred a more conventional mom. But not me. I had a conventional mom. By comparison, Hanni was a movie star with a penchant for taking to dinner any kid who happened to be listening to her jazz records or hanging with her sons.

In seventh grade I wrote a bad sports page parody for an English class. And it was Hanni who took this feeble effort up, praising me for its silly content and for this mysterious thing she called "potential."

This was not a word much heard in my own home, a loving home certainly but a place where I was told that my eyes would go bad from reading.

Hanni's criticisms were far more literate. In fact, I still own a dictionary she inscribed, "To a great future writer. Use this and you'll be even greater."

With the advent of the Nixon years, Hanni moved to Italy and married an Italian, a wonderful man named Emilio Cola, and together they shared a huge apartment in the center of Rome. I showed up there in my mid-20s driving a decrepit Austin Mini van with a pretty Scottish fiancee in tow.

At her insistence, we ended up living below them in an apartment she was minding for a friend. Like everything she did, it was all so effortless. She was just happy to have adopted children under her roof, a pair of grateful paupers who would never forget this kindness.

We kept in touch over the years. She and Emilio eventually left Rome for Maryland to be close to her boys and their growing families.

I'd call and they would visit. I once met them for coffee in a transit lounge at LAX. Another time she came bearing inscribed and carefully chosen art books for my children.

A few years ago, after not hearing from her for months, I called. It was a cold Sunday and I was sitting in my backyard under gray skies. Crows cawed in the big avocado trees as we talked, Hanni and I.

She said that she was about to take "a last trip" to Italy, to the village north of Spoletto where Emilio was born. I questioned her word choice, but she insisted that she wasn't getting any younger. Which surprised me because I always thought of her as ageless.

Then she said, "You know, I always thought of you as a son."

"Funny," I said, "I always thought of you as my mother."

I last spoke with her a year ago on New Year's Day. I heard through another stray, my friend Romi, that Hanni had Alzheimer's, a disease affecting 5 million Americans, robbing another person of life and memory every 72 seconds.

"My boy!" she said, sounding young and happy. "Tell me, did you ever get married?"

The brain hits a gap like a missing trestle.

"Yes," I said. "And we have three children."

"I bet that they are as sweet and handsome as you," she said, my heart breaking.

"They're far better, Hanni," I said, before coming back to the moment, to a blanket she was knitting, only she couldn't remember for who.

She was feeling fantastic, she told me, Maryland looked lovely in fall and did I ever get a newspaper job because I was such a good writer.

Yes, I had and partly because of her and because of how she relentlessly pushed me toward the one occupation that seemed clearly out of reach to a son of immigrants. And she did it with grace and style, like a countess in pictures, this person who accidentally taught me everything I'd ever need to know about encouraging children.

We talked about her grandkids and about Emilio, who continued to look after her like the great gentleman he is.

Finally, faltering over facts and knowing it, after forgetting entire life-segments she recalled the long-past day she showed me how to work one of her expensive Japanese cameras, letting me snap away at the family collie, giving me a kind of freedom that I found nowhere else.

"I am so tired," she said finally in a voice that was all lazy long vowels and all her own, a voice that went silent two weeks ago everywhere but in the memories of those lucky enough to have known her.

"Goodbye, son," she said, ending the call.

Goodbye, Mom.

LaVergne, TN USA
12 May 2010
182546LV00002B/4/P